SAY IT TO GOD

SAY IT TO GOD

In search of prayer

The Archbishop of Canterbury's
Lent Book 2018

Luigi Gioia

B L O O M S B U R Y

LONDON · OXFORD · NEW YORK · NEW DELHI · SYDNEY

Bloomsbury Continuum
An imprint of Bloomsbury Publishing Plc

50 Bedford Square
London
WC1B 3DP
UK

1385 Broadway
New York
NY 10018
USA

www.bloomsbury.com

Bloomsbury, Continuum and the Diana logo are trademarks of Bloomsbury Publishing Plc

First published 2017

British Library Cataloguing-in-Publication Data
A catalogue record for this book is available from the British Library.

ISBN:	PB:	9781472941756
	EPDF:	9781472941770
	EPUB:	9781472941763

2 4 6 8 10 9 7 5 3 1

Printed and bound in Great Britain by CPI Group (UK) Ltd, Croydon CR0 4YY

To find out more about our authors and books visit www.bloomsbury.com. Here you will find extracts, author interviews, details of forthcoming events and the option to sign up for our newsletters.

To Pauline Matarasso
For her friends a grace

To Bram and Peter
Certainty wells up within

CONTENTS

CONTENTS

FOREWORD

'Lord, teach us to pray.' These words of Jesus' disciples still resonate today. If we're honest, most of us would admit that prayer is not always easy, or enjoyable, and rarely comes naturally. We struggle with distractions, anxious thoughts and commitments. This book agrees! Prayer is tough. And the author does not try and give easy solutions. Instead, he takes us on a journey through great prayers from Scripture. The Psalms. The prayers of Old Testament prophets. But most of all, the prayers of Jesus. In the prayers of Jesus we discover our identity as children of God. We discover that prayer is not about us making efforts to knock on the door of a God too busy or distant to listen, but instead, that it is responding to a God who has already started the conversation with us. A God who wants nothing more than to spend time with us, help us grow, and surprise us.

Surprises are not always welcome. Sometimes the God we find in prayer is not the Santa-like God we wish he was. This God stretches us, challenges us and leads on unexpected paths. Luigi Gioia encourages us to respond to God's prompting, to face what gets in our way and to follow with child-like trust to explore a new way of being with God: to pray as, and with, Jesus, in freedom and trust. This book is therefore a perfect companion for Lent: a book to lead us through an examination of our lives, of its priorities, and to encourage us to hear the God who is already speaking. The final chapter captures the book beautifully: when it comes to prayer, keep it simple, keep it short, keep it real. And as we bring the whole of ourselves before God, he answers the prayer we started with — 'Lord, teach us to pray.'

++*Justin Cantuar*

Lambeth Palace

January 2017

ANY SCRAP OF WOOD

What is prayer really about? Not prayers, but prayer, not just saying things to God but touching God or rather being touched by him. What does an authentic prayer, a prayer that truly relies on the power of the resurrection, look like?

We should beware of our search for the best place, for the ideal conditions and for the perfect way to pray. This might lead us to forget a basic law of Christian prayer: *prayer is always already there, already going on in our heart, wherever we are, whatever we do, whatever our feelings.* The moment we realize this, we are praying. Great saints have often spoken of prayer being like breathing or having to become like breathing; that is something that should stay with us always.

Here I want to share a personal story.

I am seventeen, my faith has just come alive, I have discovered the Psalms and fallen in love with them, and have just read a wonderful book on prayer. So I try to enter into the habit of praying daily, or having my daily 'quiet time' as some people nicely call it.

And, well, it works! The five minutes a day I had decided to devote to prayer soon seem too short: they become fifteen, twenty, twenty-five minutes. I add five more minutes every day and I am not bored, I love it, it gives me so much peace, so much joy.

Those first lucky days, for a reason I do not remember, I had my home all to myself, so I could enjoy all the silence and the peace I wanted. But this blessed time was not going to last . . . I have three siblings, younger than me, the little one was two or three at the time – love them to pieces, but they could be so annoying, bless them.

So imagine the scene: I shut myself in my room, I sit on a chair, I read a psalm, re-read it, a sentence strikes me, I close my eyes and try to repeat it gently with my heart. My siblings are playing hide and seek, one of them is unhappy about something, they start arguing. The little one starts crying and comes banging at my door: so frustrating . . . I still try to keep focused, but am increasingly angry, exasperation mounts and at one point I end up shouting at my siblings to shut up, not once but several times, until, discouraged and ridden with guilt for losing my temper, I give up!

This scene occurs two or three times until, at the end of that week, I talk about the experience with a Benedictine monk. In the course of that conversation I receive an unforgettable lesson about prayer. As I vent to him my frustration and ask forgiveness for having got angry, he tells me the story of a Christian in Vietnam during a time of persecution. He was arrested because of his faith and spent several years in the tiniest cell, impossibly overcrowded with robbers, murderers and other criminals.

When, decades later, he was finally released, he said that prayer, deep prayer of the heart, had never left him in that prison and that, far from distracting him, noise, discomfort, shouting and every sort of misery he had suffered there had become the fuel of his prayer – not an obstacle, but the medium through which he learnt how to pray. So, this Benedictine monk ended up saying to me: 'the test that your prayer is authentic is learning *how to turn everything into prayer*'. '*Any scrap of wood is good to feed fire,*' he told me. This was the great lesson of my life about prayer.

Let us think about this by questioning our preconceived ideas about prayer. How often do we abandon all attempt to pray in certain places, situations or contexts because we think that prayer is about focus, about having the right feelings, being in the right mood, creating the ideal conditions and having a lot of free time. Here is a litany of the obstacles to prayer: I don't have time; I am constantly surrounded by city, noise, people; I am stressed and under pressure; I am angry, annoyed, frustrated; I feel depressed.

What if we could understand noise not as that *despite* which we pray, *against which* we pray, but that *out of which* we pray? What if anger, jealousy, frustration – all those feelings that overwhelm each one of us several times a day – what if such feelings not only ceased to be an obstacle to prayer but became the scraps of wood that feed our prayer, that keep the fire of prayer burning?

Try this: each time I feel angry, I express my anger to God, I tell God why I am angry and with whom. Is this not prayer? Each time I am frustrated or discouraged, I tell God how and why. Again: is this not prayer? Each time something has hurt me, something pains me, I tell it to God, I simply say it, *to God*. And just in the same way, when something has given me a great joy, when I have succeeded in something and am happy about it, I take a few seconds to thank the Lord: is this not prayer too? Start doing this and you might end up praying a hundred times a day, and if you add up all these scraps, you might discover that you have spent much more time in prayer than you would have done in the best of your quiet times.

Never should we think that we have to overcome our anger first, or our frustration first, before we can pray. It can be difficult to believe it, but God is sincerely, deeply interested in each of our thoughts, the good ones and the bad ones, in every one of our feelings, the nice ones and the mean ones: all of them!

Of course, the obvious question here is: what is it then that turns them into prayer? When is it that anger is only anger, and when does it become prayer? Or when is pain only pain? Or when is lust only lust (because yes, lust too can become prayer)? Or when is hatred only hatred, and when does it become prayer?

Wait a moment! Have you said hatred? Hatred that becomes prayer? Is this not pushing things a bit too far? Well, listen to this: *I hate them with perfect hatred*.[1] This is not Sauron of Mordor, this is the book of Psalms, the collection of prayers God himself taught to the Israelites. What makes this terrible sentence a prayer?

Well, only one thing, the very same thing that transformed into a prayer the most poignant cry of pain ever to have resounded on earth: *My God, my God, why have you forsaken me?*[2] What makes this scream not just a cry of pain or even a blasphemy but a prayer? The answer is *My God, my God*.

[1] Ps. 139.22.
[2] Ps. 22.1.

This is the ultimate secret of prayer, the philosopher's stone that turns every possible feeling, good or bad, nice or mean, into the gold of prayer: neither focus, nor perfect silence, nor inner peace, nor a lot of free time. The ultimate secret of prayer lies wholly in this *My God, my God!* I say it to God, I present it to God, I am always with God and know God is always with me.

BLESSED CRISIS

It's sad to have to acknowledge this, but the access route to prayer is often need. There comes a moment when we have our backs to the wall, we experience our own frailty, our impotence, with nowhere to go and no one to turn to. In this crisis, the difficulties we go through, the helplessness we feel, become unsustainable. This is when we remember the Lord, we venture a plea, a request, perhaps in tears, with an intensity never before experienced. It is sad because it shows that God exists for us only when we need him: we knew he was waiting for us, always ready, always available, but we ignored him. We allowed ourselves to be grabbed by endless activities, we lacked the motivation to pause even for a moment and to put ourselves in his presence, freely. We come back to the Lord only when the circumstances of life force us to do so.

We go back to the Lord the way the prodigal son returns to the Father: as a last recourse. Perhaps we are caught in an irreconcilable conflict and see no escape.

Maybe, misled by one whim or another, we have completely lost our way. Or we have put all our hopes and happiness in a job, a business or a relationship, and when the job disappoints, the business fails, the relationship goes through a crisis, then the meaning of life crumbles with them. We have shrunk our horizon to something that is short-lived, *because the present form of this world is passing away.*[1] We built our house on sand and the first gale, the first rainstorm, has weakened its foundations and now it threatens to collapse.

The prayer of need, the prayer we revert to as our last resort, is a demonstration of our fundamental selfishness, of our little faith. As long as we did not need the Lord we did not care about him. We might have fulfilled our religious duties, but we did not keep him in our thoughts, our heart or our desires.

Yet we have to acknowledge that the prayer of need has at least one advantage: it is authentic, it brings us back to our truth, to our fundamental dependence on the Lord; it is an opportunity to turn the crisis into *kairos*, into a favourable time, a *day of salvation.*[2]

This is why the Lord does not despise it; instead he gladly welcomes it, as the father opens his arms to

[1] 1 Cor. 7.31.
[2] 2 Cor. 6.2.

the prodigal son, or as Jesus welcomes Peter's timid confession of faith when the crowd leaves in dismay, unable to commit to the leap of faith required to accept Christ's flesh as food and his blood as drink:

> Because of this many of his disciples turned back and no longer went about with him. So Jesus asked the twelve, 'Do you also wish to go away?' Simon Peter answered him, 'Lord, to whom can we go? You have the words of eternal life. We have come to believe and know that you are the Holy One of God'.[3]

Christians who resort to prayer, even as a last option, are already way ahead of the crowd, already have a bit of faith; in their heart, there already shines a glimmer of hope. The people had come to Jesus to ask for earthly bread and when they do not get it, they start looking elsewhere, refusing to widen their horizon, to understand that there is a food for the heart even more necessary than that needed by the body. This food is our relationship with Christ, our becoming one with him, dwelling in him because he dwells in us, *praying without ceasing*,[4] *incessantly*.[5]

[3] Jn 6.66–9.
[4] Lk. 18.1.
[5] 1 Thess. 5.17.

The crowd lives *according to the flesh, it sets its minds on the things of the flesh.*[6] Jesus himself is clear: *You are looking for me, not because you saw signs, but because you ate your fill of the loaves.*[7] The disciples themselves fail to understand Jesus, they too fail to see the signs, their eyes will stay closed until the splendour of the resurrection opens them once and for all. They too deserve Jesus' rebuke: despite having witnessed two multiplications of the loaves, they were still talking among themselves about having no bread, and Jesus sharply reprimands them: 'Why are you talking about having no bread? Do you still not perceive or understand? Are your hearts hardened? Do you have eyes, and fail to see? Do you have ears, and fail to hear? And do you not remember?'[8]

Christians are no different from the 'crowd': they neither perceive nor understand, they have eyes but fail to see, ears but fail to hear. In times of crisis, however, at the crossroads of despair and hope, they mysteriously discover themselves able to dare. As they anxiously wonder where help will come from, they venture *to raise their eyes to the mountains* and proclaim: *Our help comes from the Lord, he made heaven and earth.*[9]

[6] Rom. 8.5.
[7] Jn 6.26.
[8] Mk 8.17–18.
[9] Ps. 121.1–2.

Hence, however timid, however imperfect, however motivated by the absence of any other option, by its being the only alternative to despair or cynicism, the prayer of need, the prayer of last resort, becomes a formidable springboard, the crossroads at which life takes a new direction: *I will go to my father and say:*[10] *To whom can I go?*[11] Something in my heart tells me that *you are my God and that besides you there is no God.*[12]

Therefore, crisis and need often serve as doors to prayer. They are times of truth because we are reminded of our fundamental condition as creatures before our Creator:

> To you I lift up my eyes, you who dwell in heaven . . . Our eyes look to the Lord our God till he has mercy on us. Have mercy upon us, O Lord, have mercy upon us, for we have had more than enough of contempt. Our soul has had more than its fill of the scorn of those who are at ease, of the contempt of the proud.[13]

The scorn and contempt that humiliate us come from the absurdity of the circumstances that imprison

[10] Lk. 15.18.
[11] Cf. Jn 6.68.
[12] Cf. Ps 86.8.
[13] Ps. 123.1–4.

us and cut off all escape routes. Life brings us back cyclically to moments like these, with a regularity in which it is hard not to detect some sort of law of spiritual life. Not that the Lord directs events in order to engineer such crises in our lives every time we forget him. On the contrary, he created us to live in peaceful familiarity with him, he placed us in a garden where there was no danger, where there were only opportunities to recognize a sign of his blessing in every tree, every fruit, every blade of grass, and in each other. He created a transparent world where everything proclaimed his glory, his goodness, his love for us.

If creation suddenly became opaque it was because a veil fell on our eyes. If *scorn and contempt*,[14] pain, suffering, disease and death, appeared in our lives it was because we let the serpent into our garden, we preferred the creature to the Creator, we became jealous of God. Wary of him, we followed our own devices, we refused to recognize that we are creatures owing everything to the giver of all life and of all good. We set off for a distant land, the land of oblivion, we turned our back on light and preferred darkness, and having abandoned God we found ourselves deaf and

[14] Ps. 123.4.

blind: 'Do you still not perceive or understand? Are your hearts hardened? Do you have eyes, and fail to see? Do you have ears, and fail to hear? And do you not remember?'[15]

No wonder that, having become blind, we stumble at every rock, every obstacle on the way to life. The regularity with which crises recur in our lives is the consequence of the helplessness into which we fell when we wandered away from the Lord. Even a Christian who tries to pray regularly does not escape this law. Like Martha, we are busy doing too many things,[16] our relationship with the Lord is side-lined, we do not find time to dwell with him, in his presence. So we grow cold, we become spiritually inert, until a crisis occurs or some difficulty crops up: only then do we open our eyes and discover how far we have drifted away from the Lord. Then, and only then, do we feel the need to take refuge in the shadow of his wings and, seeking forgiveness, resort to him with all our heart and being.

This alternation between oblivion and transient conversions can last for years. The Lord deals out an infinite treasure of patience, kindness and generosity to

[15] Mk 8.17–18.
[16] Lk. 10.41.

lead us to authentic repentance and conversion.[17] Most of the time, however, as soon as the difficulty wanes, as soon as the crisis is over, the newly found fervour in prayer cools down again. Yet there also comes a day when we manage to cling to the Lord, to dwell with him even when things get better, even when the crisis is over or the need is felt less acutely; a day comes when we finally choose the best part: we sit at the Lord's feet to watch and pray without getting tired.[18]

It is the story of the Song of Songs, in which the beloved alternates between surges of enthusiasm for her lover and spells of indolence and laziness.

Despite the many proofs of the Lord's love and loyalty, when he knocks at the door the beloved still delays surrendering to him: *I had put off my garment; how could I put it on again? I had bathed my feet; how could I soil them?* And when, too late, she opens the door, the Lord has disappeared: *I opened to my beloved, but my beloved had turned and was gone.*[19]

Of course the Lord did not disappear in retaliation, but to educate the desire of the beloved, to get her

[17] Rom. 2.4.
[18] Cf. Lk. 18.1.
[19] Song 5.3,6.

out of her paralysing indolence, to introduce her into a true and passionate search for God. Through this education, there comes a day when the bride finally lets herself be sealed on the Lord's heart, a day when her love becomes stronger than death: the waters of forgetfulness and of laziness can no longer put out the fire of this love.[20]

True, eager, heartfelt prayer, a prayer in which we truly come into the Lord's presence, whether it be triggered by need or crisis, always becomes an opportunity to return to the Lord. And, at some point, thanks to this imperfect prayer we may even obtain the grace to remain in his presence, because he is our God and we belong to him, we are his children and he is our Father, we are the bride and he is the bridegroom, and because without him we can do nothing.[21]

[20] Cf. Song 8.6–7.
[21] Jn 15.5.

CLOSING THE DOOR

The prayer of crisis is not the only one that can open the door to a life of prayer, to the habit of dwelling with the Lord. There are certainly higher ways or occasions leading to the same end — notably the example of people transformed by a life of prayer, or the writings of saints or authors who have received the gift of initiating others into prayer. We can reach the Lord by a variety of paths.

But whatever the occasion that awakens in us the need or the desire to pray, it always springs from a previous gift, a call. Even though most of the time we are deaf to this call, the Lord ceaselessly invites us, provokes us, waits for us.

Scripture brims with these pleas:

Listen! I am standing at the door, knocking; if you hear my voice and open the door, I will come in to you and eat with you, and you with me.[1]

Come to me, all you that are weary and are carrying heavy burdens, and I will give you rest.[2]

[1] Rev. 3.20.
[2] Mt. 11.28.

All day long I have held out my hands to a disobedient and unwilling people.[3]

I will persuade her, bring her into the wilderness and speak tenderly to her.[4]

Arise, my love, my fair one, and come away.[5]

Open to me, my sister, my love, my dove, my perfect one.[6]

All these pleas echo the invitations that never cease to resound in our heart whenever we are overwhelmed by the beauty of creation or experience the fullness of a moment of silence; whenever a desire inexplicably springs up in our heart or we struggle with a feeling of dissatisfaction that nothing can fill or still.

Starting to pray, even tentatively, is like finding a new friend: we want to spend more time with him and we find a space for this almost naturally even in the midst of our busy lives. In the same way, once we have tasted the friendship of the Lord, carving a space for prayer in our lives seems a natural step. *Taste and see that the Lord is good, blessed are those who take refuge in him:*[7] as we greet this new experience of the Lord's

[3] Isa. 65.2; cf. Rom. 10.21.
[4] Hos. 2.14.
[5] Song 2.10.
[6] Song 5.2.
[7] Ps. 34.8.

presence in our hearts, *sweeter than honey to our mouth*,[8] the commitment to find some moments of our day to devote to prayer becomes a joy.

Carving a little space for prayer in our lives! This is what Jesus suggests when he says: 'Whenever you pray, go into your room, close the door and pray to your Father who is in secret; and your Father who sees in secret will reward you.'[9]

An almost two-thousand-year-old spiritual tradition in Christianity has amassed a treasure of wisdom to help us build a conducive environment for prayer, to allow us to dwell in God's presence throughout our activities; in short, to preserve the freedom that is ours as children of God, and which includes the freedom to pray. Ensuring we are free to pray is often a great challenge for Christians and requires some imagination.

The logic of our modern society is dominated by the dread of emptiness, or what appears to be emptiness to people who have never learnt the value of silence or meditation, of spending time alone with themselves. Our modern means of communication render us reachable always and everywhere. In the past

[8] Ps. 119.103.
[9] Mt. 6.6.

a journey by train or by car offered an opportunity for rest, solitude, prayer, contemplation of nature, or reflection. Today these journeys are filled with phone calls or messaging. Nothing wrong with that of course. Our aim is not to isolate ourselves from others, but to prevent the dread of emptiness (*horror vacui*), the vanity and the rejection of God that unfortunately exist in our world from swallowing us up too.

Jesus teaches that when we pray we should enter our room and shut the door, meaning that we should try to create and preserve a favourable atmosphere for prayer. True, we can protect ourselves from most distractions and still be unable to gather ourselves in God's presence and pray. Those wise Christians who lived in Egypt in the fourth and fifth century, commonly known as the Desert Fathers, knew this law of the spiritual life all too well and declared that even in the desert a monk keeps the world in his heart.

'Closing the door' therefore means using some imagination to carve out the space and atmosphere most conducive to spending time in the Lord's presence. It is not only about finding the right space for prayer – 'your room' as the Gospel puts it – but especially about learning how to deal with time, or rather with the lack of it.

Undeniably there are periods of our life when duties colonise our days and time for prayer seems impossible to find. But should this become habitual we might need to review the balance of our lives. Christians should never let their work or activities fill their day to the point where no time is left for the one truly necessary thing.

This is the teaching of Jesus' parable of the sower or rather of the seed.[10] In the Gospel this seed is the word but it can also be also interpreted as the desire to welcome God's presence and action in us.

All day long the Lord sows in our heart this seed of the desire to listen to his word, to be united with him, to join him in friendship, to be in communion with him. Most of the time we do not pay attention to it because we are careless and in haste and it is easily snatched away. At other times we joyfully welcome this seed, this desire for God, this call to prayer, but our inconstancy does not allow it to take root in our hearts and the initial enthusiasm quickly fades away. Or it happens that the seed of this desire of God is choked by worldly worries, by the seduction of wealth and by other passions.

[10] Cf. Mk 4:1–20.

To grow and to yield its fruit, the seed of prayer needs a favourable soil. This good soil, as we have seen, is the belief that God is sincerely, deeply interested in each of our thoughts, the good and the bad, in every one of our feelings, the nice and the mean. Each of these thoughts and feelings can be a springboard to turn our hearts to him, even just for a fleeting moment, when we say it to God, as Jesus did.

This good soil also is the growing joy and peace we find in taking a little time every day in which we try to dwell in the Father's presence, even though this is often difficult, and renew our trust in him, reminding ourselves that he takes care of us:

Do not worry, saying, 'What will we eat?' or 'What will we drink?' or 'What will we wear?' For it is the Gentiles who strive for all these things; your heavenly Father knows that you need all of them. Strive first for the kingdom of God and his righteousness, and all these things will be given to you as well. So do not worry about tomorrow, for tomorrow will bring worries of its own. Today's trouble is enough for today.[11]

[11] Mt. 6.31–34.

A PRESENCE WE DISCOVER IN US

The Lord himself opens a space for prayer in our hearts. He invites us there, to be alone with him, to find rest in him: 'Come away to a deserted place all by yourselves and rest a while.'[1] He awakes in us a longing to see our life centred on him. Lodged in the deepest part of our heart there is a desire for prayer, one can even say a *need* for prayer. We have to acknowledge, to detect this desire, this need: 'Prayer is the answer to our soul's need for worship.'[2]

Here, however, we come up against a paradox: we have this desire, this deep need for prayer, yet we experience it constantly as hard. There is something in us that feels uneasy with prayer and shies away from it, that repeatedly finds excuses for putting it off to another day. It is important to understand why.

Let us begin with Jesus' teaching on worship in this wonderful sentence from John's Gospel: 'The

[1] Mk 6.31.
[2] Matta el Meskin, *L'Esperienza di Dio nella Preghiera* (Bose: Qiqajon, 1999), 30.

23

hour is coming, and is now here, when the true worshippers will worship the Father in spirit and truth, for the Father seeks such as these to worship him.'[3]

The hour is coming, and is now here.[4] The first feature of prayer is that it is *urgent*. It is for today, it is for now; we cannot, we should not postpone it. This is the biblical way of saying that prayer is the most import-ant thing of all, not only the thing our soul desires but also that which all humanity, indeed the whole of creation, desperately needs. Humanity, the world, creation, *groan in travail*: 'We know that the whole of creation has been groaning in labour pains until now; and not only creation, but we ourselves, who have the first fruits of the Spirit, groan inwardly.'[5] The spirit of children in us has to be freed and revealed: 'For the creation waits with eager longing for the revealing of the children of God . . . in the hope that it will be set free from its bondage to decay and will obtain the freedom of the glory of the children of God.'[6] That which Paul calls the spirit of children

[3] Jn 4.23.
[4] Ibid.
[5] Rom. 8.22–23.
[6] Rom. 8.20–21.

24

is the truest, the deepest, the most important thing in us; in its liberation lies the only rest and the only peace for our restless soul: 'the glorious freedom of the children of God'![7]

The Father seeks such as these to worship him.[8] The second feature of prayer is that it is *a gift from the Father*, a gift he is giving us here and now: the Father wants, desires, seeks prayer. This means that the soul, humanity, the world, creation, are not alone in needing prayer but the Father too seeks it. This need for prayer that we feel is in fact a pull coming from the Father. Indeed, as Jesus says, *no one comes to me unless the Father draws him*,[9] and the gift of worship we receive is *the living water* that Jesus promises will rise in the hearts of those who believe in him. It is the *murmur* the martyr Ignatius felt as a prisoner on his way to Rome where he was going to be devoured by lions: 'There is in me living water that murmurs: come to the Father.'[10] It is the *deepest voice* of our heart that coincides with the voice of the Spirit within us that cries out *Abba, Father.*[11] It is *a gift, a grace*, the result

[7] Cf. Rom. 8.21.
[8] Jn 4.23.
[9] Jn 6.44.
[10] Ignatius of Antioch, *Romans* 7.2.
[11] Gal. 4.6.

of the action of the Father and of the Holy Spirit, but also and above all of Christ, the *risen Christ*.

True worshippers will worship the Father in spirit and truth.[12] The third feature of prayer is that it is *in spirit*, that is, from the deepest part of our being, from our heart. Prayer is true, is authentic, only if it arises from our spirit. It is at this juncture that we need to explore the link between prayer and resurrection.

Easy enough to say, but having access to the deepest part of our heart, the heart from which alone true prayer arises, is far from easy. We have a rebellious heart, a closed heart, a sick heart, as Scripture constantly reminds us. Every morning we are warned not to harden our heart.[13] And we know only too well how tightly our heart is closed to God, just as it is closed to our brothers and sisters. Nor is our heart hardened and closed only to God and others. Were this the case, were our heart closed only to the Father and to others, we might still be able to survive. The tragedy is that our heart is at odds with ourselves too, it blames us too; as John says in his first letter: *our heart condemns us.*[14]

[12] Jn 4.23.
[13] Ps. 95.8.
[14] Jn 3.20.

This means that trying to penetrate our heart, trying to get in touch with the deepest part of our soul, with our *spirit*, can be rather unappealing. It is like going back into a prison, a gloomy space closed and bolted in which we have shut ourselves, prisoners of a voice that accuses and blames us. We are locked in our hearts exactly as were the trembling disciples, who stayed huddled behind closed doors before the resurrection of Jesus: *the doors of the place where the disciples had met were locked for fear of the Jewish leaders.*[15] Fear was the key that locked their door, the same fear that keeps us hidden today behind our inner walls.

Religiosity is no help against this. It can even add a further layer to these already thick walls. There is a certain familiarity with Scripture, with prayers, in short, with religion, that can make us impervious to the action of the Lord. The disciples could live side by side with Jesus and yet remain fearful and *of little faith.*[16] Our doors are closed because at some point we turned inward, and, our hope having forgotten how to dare, we have come to believe that God is powerless or has abandoned us. Discouraged by a resistance to God that we meet in ourselves and did

[15] Jn 20.19.
[16] Cf. Mt. 6.30, 8.26; 14.31.

not expect, we give up. We wanted to be more generous, more open in our service of the Lord, but we fail: discouragement, lassitude, resignation and cynicism close our doors.

And yet, precisely at this juncture, just when we too, like the disciples after Jesus' death, have lost all hope and locked the doors, we might be visited by the risen Lord. Authentic prayer can only spring from the depths of our hearts; but what if our hearts are closed and fear prevents us from opening the doors? The good news is that Christ, now risen, can come through closed doors to deliver us. Closed doors are not a barrier to him: *Although the doors were shut, Jesus came and stood among them and said, 'Peace be with you!'* [17]

This takes us into the real meaning of resurrection and its link to prayer. Resurrection is not about going through wooden doors or walls: this would be magic. Resurrection is this new capacity that Jesus has acquired to reach us wherever we might be lost or imprisoned. *Resurrexi et adhuc tecum sum*, 'Risen, I am with you always', runs a wonderful Latin Gregorian antiphon of Easter – a sentence that exquisitely captures the essence of the resurrection. The most insistent promise and assurance God utters in the Old

[17] Jn 20.26.

Testament is this: *I will be with you, I am with you.*[18] Jesus is the fulfilment of this promise. His name is *Emmanuel, that is God with us*, but only with the resurrection is this promise realized. Only then can Jesus be everywhere at all times in the power of his Spirit so that neither distance, nor darkness, nor even our wish to flee away from him, can escape the reach of his love and his presence any more.

> Where can I go from your spirit? Or where can I flee from your presence? If I ascend to heaven, you are there; if I make my bed in Sheol, you are there. If I take the wings of the morning and settle at the furthest limits of the sea, even there your hand shall lead me, and your right hand shall hold me fast. If I say, 'Surely the darkness shall cover me, and the light around me become night', even the darkness is not dark to you; the night is as bright as the day, for darkness is as light to you.[19]

Yes, the risen Christ can reach down to the deepest corners where we are hiding, prisoners of our loneliness, our fears, our anxieties, our despair, our depressions, our cynicism, our shame, and there he

[18] Cf. Exod. 3.12; Deut. 20.1; Isa. 43.2; etc.
[19] Ps. 139.7–12.

shows us his hands and his side. This is an important gesture. It is Jesus' way of saying to us: 'I know what you are suffering because I shared it. I know your sadness because I felt it, I know your feeling of having being abandoned by God because I screamed it, I know your loneliness because I was betrayed by all my friends. But thanks to me all this suffering has become a source of life, light, peace, and joy, and it reopens the doors, it abolishes the walls, it restores the relationship with the Father.'

Our doors are closed because we are afraid of the Father, just like the prodigal son who travelled to a far country, and because we are afraid of each other. Yet Jesus comes, wherever we are, he reaches us, we discover him among us, in us, and we hear him as he repeats to us his reassuring 'Peace to you'. 'Do not let your heart be troubled, do not be afraid, it is I.'[20]

Our life of prayer begins when we finally experience this presence of the risen Lord, which brings peace, joy, freedom, hope – when we finally hear him saying in the depths of our hearts: 'Peace to you'. This is why resurrection and prayer are inseparable: the resurrection is not a reality that we see, but a presence

[20] Cf. Jn 14.1

that we discover – not outside us, but within, in our inmost being. And thus prayer becomes a matter of learning to wait in faith and in hope for the risen Lord to enter into our locked selves, just as he entered the locked room where the apostles waited in discouragement and fear.

So *the hour is coming, and is now here, when the true worshippers will worship the Father in spirit and in truth.*[21] It has come because Christ is risen, because we are no longer alone, locked in ourselves, because our hearts have become the place where we can at last find a saving presence, a presence that gives us peace. Prayer is now the space where we welcome the fruits of the resurrection.

[21] Jn 4.23.

SAVING TIME

Relationship with time is one of the cornerstones of Christian experience. When faith in God dawns in our hearts, when we discover the Lord present and active in our lives, then our relation to time changes. Scripture refers to this change using two different Greek words for time: *chronos* and *kairos*. The moment we enter into a loving relationship with the Lord, the moment we start praying, time is transformed from *chronos* into *kairos*.

Chronos is the time measured by the stars, the seasons and the watches devised to manage it as effectively as possible. *Chronos* is like the overseer of a galley beating out on a huge drum the rhythm to be kept up by the galley slaves. *Chronos* is relentless: an hour is an hour and when it is over, it is over. We have a limited number of days to live, and when the last arrives, there is no escape. *Chronos* is cold, mechanical. Its unflinching regularity admits of no exceptions, and combined with the variability of our psychological perception of time it constantly mocks us: whenever an activity is pleasant, time always flies too fast; but whenever we are in pain, toiling with something, distressed by something, then time never passes, minutes last for ever! *Chronos* is both inflexible and whimsical; it exposes our vulnerability and is the main ally of our greatest enemy, death. *Chronos* is death a drop at a time in the form of each and every instant, which, as soon as it has started, is already gone. *Chronos* is a prison: it does not lead anywhere, it reproduces the same cycle relentlessly. It has no direction, it pursues no aim, it is absurd, meaningless.

Kairos, on the other hand, is the Lord himself who breaks into *chronos* and disrupts its blind monotony and its cyclical nature. As soon as the Lord enters history he inaugurates a new beginning, a new creation, which rescues our lives from the cyclical nature of *chronos* by giving us a direction, a meaning, a purpose. When the Word became flesh; when Jesus promised to dwell with us in his word and in the community of believers; when he rose from the dead and sent his Spirit into our hearts: in each of these instances time was changed and it became the place where the Kingdom of God breaks in and where we are granted a foretaste of the life to come.

Whenever we welcome the word with faith, whenever we welcome the presence and action of the Lord in our lives, whenever we pray, our time is transfigured: it is no longer one more passing instant to be endured; instead it becomes a chosen time, a bridge between heaven and earth, between present and future, it becomes patient waiting, the watchfulness of the gospel: it becomes hope.

Unfortunately, even though *chronos* no longer exists, even though the advent of the Kingdom of God has transformed every moment into an occasion of grace and an opportunity for salvation, we are still prevented from welcoming this liberation by our lack of faith and by our blindness. Although our chains were broken and the gates of hell torn apart, we remain stubbornly crouched in the darkness of our cell, not daring to leave our prison. Paul multiplied his pleas for us to acknowledge and welcome God's time, this time of salvation, the favourable time inaugurated by the resurrection of Christ:

Brothers and sisters, the appointed time has grown short; from now on, let those who have wives be as though they had none, and those who mourn as though they were not mourning, and those who rejoice as though they were not rejoicing, and those who buy as though they had no possessions, and those who deal with the world as though they had no dealings with it. For the present form of this world is passing away.[1]

This *kairos* is short, urgent, stretched towards the coming world. What we are experiencing now is temporary and must be put at the service of the life to come. If we do not want to become slaves of *chronos* we must keep a certain distance between us and our activities so as to see everything from the viewpoint of the world to come. To maintain this distance, to perceive and manage time as the break-in space where the Lord is coming to establish his Kingdom, to *deal with the world as though we had no dealings with it*, we have to be watchful, asking continually for his coming, seeking the justice of his Kingdom; in short, we have to *pray*.

Only by a serious commitment to daily prayer can *we rescue our time*.[2] We talk about 'saving time', meaning that we try to use it more strategically, so as to be able to do more and do it better. But time needs to be 'saved' also in the sense that it needs to be 'rescued'

[1] Cor. 7.29–31.
[2] Eph. 5.16; Col. 4.5.

from spinning on its own axis and pulling us into a spiral that leads nowhere. When Paul talks about *rescuing time* he uses the Greek verb *exagorazomai*, which elsewhere in his writings indicates the action through which Christ saves us, through which he *rescued us so that we might receive adoption as children*.[3] Literally, this word means 'buy back', 'take possession of something that had once belonged to us, but that we had lost'. Only when we stop, only when we get into our room and close the door for a little while, only when we pray, does time cease to elude us, to control us, and we can escape from its coercion. Only then are we offered the chance to *rescue* it, to take it back, to transform it, or better, to let it be transformed by the Lord into a time of salvation, into a *kairos*.

There are many ways in which we save time in this way, in which we *rescue* our time. Repentance and mercy offer a good example. When the evening comes, if I put myself prayerfully in the presence of the merciful Lord to reconsider my day and ask for forgiveness for everything that went wrong, then I am *rescuing* my day, I am claiming it back. An instant of repentance is enough to rescue all the hours I spent

[3] Gal. 4.5.

forgetting or ignoring the Lord, all the hours I spent totally absorbed by my work to the point of forgetting even myself. This is something I can do in the evening, but also at mid-morning, at noon and in mid-afternoon. Or I can, little by little, learn how to do it even more often, even without interrupting my work, because just a few seconds are enough. In this way, prayer might even progressively become an underlying posture so that with time no activity, however demanding, will ever completely distract me from the Lord's presence.

Take another example. When the logic of the world becomes intrusive to the point of wanting to take over my entire day with appointments, phone calls, distractions and duties, even if these activities are good in themselves, I can refuse to let them determine the pace of my life and hinder my freedom as a child of God, choosing instead to spend even just five or ten minutes in prayer, for the Lord. The logic of the world rebels against such intransigence: the Lord can wait, whereas this phone call, this appointment, this duty is urgent. But when we forfeit the brief time of prayer we had intended to have in favour of another activity, however worthy and good, it is not the Lord that we leave waiting, it is not him that we harm, but ourselves, because we trammel our freedom as children of God. Deciding to give up or shorten an activity for the sake of prayer is an act of freedom with respect to the logic of the world, it is an act of faith in the life to come, in the fact that this world is passing away, whereas prayer and love, like the word of God, abide for ever.

St Jane Frances de Chantal supposedly said: 'Whoever finds time for God, finds it for everything else too.' Indeed, those who find time for God, those who find time for worship and prayer, become freer, are released from the logic of the passing world and participate already in Christ's kingship over time. And when *chronos* is transfigured into *kairos*, the Lord himself directs everything according to his providence down to the tiniest details of our lives, and somehow everything works better, runs more smoothly.

If the time of prayer is marred by delay, laziness or haste, this means that we still are prisoners of the logic of *chronos*, that we have not welcomed the conversion required by the Lord: 'As Jesus passed along the Sea of Galilee, he saw Simon and his brother Andrew casting a net into the lake for they were fish-ermen. And Jesus said to them, "Follow me and I will make you fishers of people." And immediately they left their nets and followed him.'[4] This invitation to conversion, to follow Jesus, is renewed every time the Spirit calls us to pray: we must then leave our nets, assemble the resources of our hearts, imagination and intelligence to welcome the presence of the Lord.

In this patient, persevering and sometimes strenuous conversion, renewed each time we *let down the nets* to respond to the Lord in prayer, day after day, our perception of time gradually changes. We realize that the time of the clock, *chronos*, is waning, while the time transfigured by the Lord's presence, the *kairos*, is increasingly present and active among us and in this way we can enjoy the wonderful privilege we have as Christians of *sanctifying* time. Then we can say: *Sun and Moon, bless the Lord. Stars of heaven, bless the Lord. Nights and days, bless the Lord. Light and darkness, bless the Lord.*[5] Sun, moon, stars are all symbols of time. This is a way of letting time become a blessing. And indeed *kairos* could be translated as 'time blessed', 'time filled with God's blessing'.

This is the best way to save time, to rescue time. This is what Jesus meant when he invited us to *be*

4 Mk 1.16–17.
5 Dan. 3.62–63, 71–72.

watchful.[6] Whenever we fend off the bondage of *chronos*, whenever we distance ourselves from clock time and from the worldly logic that governs it, whenever we welcome the *kairos*, the Kingdom of God, then indeed we save, we rescue, we sanctify time. This is why prayer is the work of sanctification of time: every second, every minute, every hour spent in prayer becomes incense pleasing to God: *Let my prayer be counted as incense before you and the lifting up of my hands as an evening sacrifice.*[7] Every moment spent in prayer becomes a proclamation of the primacy of the Lord in our lives and in history, thus hastening the coming of the Kingdom and the return of Christ in glory.

[6] Cf. Mk 13.33.
[7] Ps. 141.2.

MEANING WORDS

The new wine of prayer flows freely from the Father! *For your love is better than wine . . . we will extol your love more than wine.*[1] Wine is there to be enjoyed, to *gladden the heart of man.*[2] Enjoying wine requires skills, experience, time. People attend special courses to learn how to appreciate its texture and perfume, how to sip it, how to combine it with food. Some flavours flatter our taste straight away, but we grow tired of them very quickly. Other flavours resist us, surprise us, sometimes we even dislike them at first, not because they are bad, but because they are too good, too rich. Our taste is poor, our sensitivity needs to be trained.

Such is the new wine of prayer: it requires new wineskins,[3] new hearts, a new ability to taste. Unless the Lord gives us *a new heart*[4] we cannot pray. The

[1] Song 1.1, 4.
[2] Ps. 104.15.
[3] Mt. 9.17.
[4] Ezek. 36.26.

never-changing law of prayer, the inescapable truth of prayer is given by Paul: *We do not know how to pray*.[5] This not only applies at the beginning of our life of prayer, but becomes truer and truer as we are led deeper into it. *Saying prayers* is never new, it is even reassuringly unchanging, if a little boring. *Praying*, on the contrary, can never be taken for granted, never ceases to challenge us, never becomes a safe routine we have mastered and can keep under control.

The new wine of prayer is the Holy Spirit, poured in our hearts, alive and active in us. In our hearts the Spirit *cries*,[6] in our hearts the Spirit *sighs*,[7] threatening to burst our shrivelled, hard, tiny wineskins.

> Suppose you want to fill some sort of bag – says Augustine – and you know the bulk of what you will be given: you stretch the bag or the sack or the skin or whatever it is. You know the size of the object that you want to put in and you see that the bag is narrow so you increase its capacity by stretching it. In the same way . . . by making us desire [him], the Lord expands the soul, and by this expansion he increases its capacity.[8]

[5] Rom. 8.26.
[6] Gal. 4.6.
[7] Rom. 8.26.
[8] Augustine, *Commentary on the first letter of St John* 4.6.

A wineskin capable of widening to the measure of God's gift needs to be fairly stretchy! The gift is not *something*, the gift is God *himself*, it is his Spirit, the Gift of the Father. Our old wineskins will never stretch enough to contain wine so good and so plentiful: they will burst.

So, we do not know how to pray. We might wish to pray, hope to become prayerful people. We might wish to benefit from the quiet, the detachment, the peace that prayer is supposed to bring to our lives, but, understandably, we soon lose heart. The taste of this wine is too strong for us, our vessels are too old and small. We are like poor Nicodemus who thought he could understand Jesus without following him.[9] Nicodemus is a tragic figure. He had the humility to ask, but lacked the freedom to listen, that is to abandon his preconceptions and to let Jesus surprise him, change him, question him in return. Nobody wants to be put in the position of following the sound of the wind, without knowing where it comes from or where it goes, where it will lead us.[10]

To Nicodemus' humility in questioning Jesus, the disciples add something else: they take the risk of

[9] Jn 3.4.,3.9
[10] Jn 3.8.

45

following Jesus, of staying with him, however confusing this proves to be. They too do not understand
him – *You still do not understand?*[11] – but they stick to
him: *I believe Lord, come to help my lack of faith.*[12] Which
in the end is the crucial decision in Christian life:
whatever happens, never letting go of remaining with
the Lord, of sticking to him: *I was senseless and ignorant;
I was a brute beast before you.Yet I still stick to you: you hold
me by my right hand.*[13]

When it comes to prayer the disciples, like us, are
as sloppy as one can be, bored, more often asleep than
not, even at the most crucial moments: *Peter and his
companions were very sleepy* just when Jesus was unveiling to them his divine beauty,[14] and fully asleep when
he most needed their support.[15] Yet they were puzzled
by their master's habit of withdrawing to solitary
places, of disappearing just when people were finally
looking for him, just when he seemed to have reached
a peak of success. They were puzzled by his need to
spend time in silence, whole nights away, alone: 'In
the morning, while it was still very dark, he got up

[11] Mk 8.17.
[12] Mk 9.24.
[13] Ps. 73.22–23.
[14] Lk 9.32.
[15] Mk 14.37, 40.

and went out to a deserted place, and there he prayed. And Simon and his companions hunted for him. When they found him, they said to him, "Everyone is searching for you."[16]

What was he doing all by himself? True disciples never grow tired of being puzzled by Jesus. Something attracts them to him – something they feel, an experience they find hard to understand. The same thing that led them to leave everything and follow him when he called them.[17] Even when they grumbled, this mysterious pull kept its hold on them. Little did they know this was the Father's doing: '*Nobody comes to me unless the Father who sent me draws him.*'[18] They were caught in the gravitational field of divine life before they even knew it. 'For I, except you enthral me, never shall be free', Donne famously said.[19]

Closely interwoven with our *not knowing how to pray*, which defines our relationship with God, is this attraction we feel towards the Lord, almost despite ourselves, and certainly despite all our weaknesses, inadequacies

[16] Mk 1.35–37.
[17] Mk 1.16ff.
[18] John 6.44.
[19] John Donne, 'Holy Sonnet XIV', *The Complete English Poems*, ed. A. J. Smith (New York: Penguin, 1984), 314–15.

and betrayals. When we see Jesus needing this silence, these times of loneliness, we are filled with a yearning for something long forgotten and now covert in us, like embers under the ashes of a neglected fire. And at last we pluck up courage and, like the daring disciple, ask him to teach us how to pray: *One day Jesus was praying in a certain place. When he finished, one of his disciples said to him: 'Lord, teach us to pray.'* [20]

These pious Jewish men were not incapable of praying. They had the Psalms. They had regular times of prayer at the Synagogue. They had the wonderful habit of the *berakah*, that is of blessing the Lord throughout the day, from the moment they woke up until they went to sleep: for good and even bad news, for awe-inspiring experiences of nature such as thunder, lightning, the sight of a mountain or of the ocean, for food and wine. They had a deep sense of their dependence on God for all their joys and needs, from the greatest to the least. No aspect of everyday life was deemed too small or insignificant to serve as an occasion to thank and bless the source of all goodness, *for everything God created is good, and nothing is to be rejected if it is received with thanksgiving.* [21]

[20] Lk. 11.1.
[21] Tim. 4.4.

But there are *prayers* and there is *prayer*. We need prayers, we need the Psalms, we need to bless and thank the Lord. Our relation with the Lord rests on *prayers*, but does not take off until we are introduced into *prayer*.

However, we are entitled to be a little puzzled here. The disciples ask Jesus to teach them *to pray* and apparently Jesus answers this request by adding one more text to their prayers, giving them what we call '*the* Our Father'! And this is how we have learnt it, as one of a set of prayers to be said morning and evening. And each time it is mumbled, hurried through in our gatherings, it is as one prayer among many, one of the most important surely, but belonging to the same category as other prayers. Until one day we start paying attention to the words. We might not understand all of them, we might not be able to mean all of them, but we discover that one or other of its sentences actually speaks to us, gives voice to something which is already present in us: *your will be done, forgive us our trespasses, give us this day our daily bread* . . . We discover that these sentences touch something which matters at a very deep level, something so important that to ask it only once is not enough, that we feel compelled to ask it over and over again, meaning it more and more genuinely.

One of the most telling signs that our faith is coming alive and that our spiritual life is growing deeper is the extent to which we mean each sentence of the *Our Father* when we say it. Not only the sentences that concern us directly: our bread, our sins, our temptations – but increasingly those sentences we struggle even to understand, those that relate to the Father's name, to his kingdom, to his will . . .

Even then we have only scratched the surface. We are still praying the *Our Father* like a prayer, an increasingly eloquent, an unusually deep prayer, but still *a* prayer among others, still just one of the prayers. We are led beyond or below this surface only when we realize what happens when we are *enabled* to start this prayer, enabled to open our lips and say *Father* and even more so to say *Our Father*!

Unless the Lord unseals our lips, we cannot pray. The first words monks and nuns say each morning just after they get up, when they go to church for vigils, are these: 'Lord, open my lips' – and often they repeat the sentence three times, to make sure it sinks in, and to become more aware of its importance: *O Lord, open my lips, and my mouth will declare your praise.*[22] We

[22] Ps. 51.15.

often assume that all we need is to know what to do and how to do it – then we are left free to decide whether to implement it or not. So with Jesus: we think we only need to be told by him how to pray and start doing it. But why do we need to ask the Lord to *open our lips* then?

The truth is that Jesus' teaching reaches us only if he heals us. In the first chapter of the Gospel of Mark we hear at most four or five short sentences from Jesus' mouth, but we see him actively casting out demons, healing people from diseases, purifying someone from leprosy. Each of these illnesses illustrates one of the crippling effects of sin on souls and bodies: we might want to follow Jesus, but we are bed-ridden or paralysed; we might want to see him, but we are blind; hear him, but we are deaf; thank him, praise him, pray to the Father who sent him, but we are dumb. Unless our tongue is loosed it cannot pray; unless our heart is freed it cannot pray. *No one can say 'Jesus is Lord' except by the Holy Spirit,*[23] nobody can say 'Father' unless the Holy Spirit who abides in the heart says it for us: *God has sent the Spirit of his Son into our hearts, crying, 'Abba! Father!'*[24]

[23] Cor. 12.3.
[24] Gal. 4.6.

Jesus is not just a master, a teacher – he is the good shepherd who takes us on his shoulders. He does not just point the way; he *is* the way. Not only does he give his life for us; we live in him. And when it comes to the *Our Father*, we can only say it because Jesus said it first, and he is saying it still. Thus, if we want to understand the *Our Father*, if we want to go beneath the surface and understand why it is not just one prayer among many, but the very heart of the mystery of prayer, we must start by seeing what it means on Jesus' lips and what happens when he says it.

SOMETHING MYSTERIOUS

We might think that, through the *Our Father*, Jesus is simply teaching us what we should ask of God and how to ask it, so that we can be sure of being listened to. This is true, but there is much more to it. Or rather it is true *because* there is more to it. All hinges on the relation between Jesus' own prayer and our prayer. What Jesus teaches us is how he himself prays.

When we look into this relation we find many layers, each deeper than the other. To each of these layers we have joined an image.

A *first layer* is that our prayer relates to Jesus because we learn it from him ('Something mysterious'). Then – *second layer* – we discover that Jesus is teaching to us his own way of praying ('Unexpected glimpses'). A *third layer* is uncovered when we realize that this way of praying is for Jesus the expression of what it means for him to be the Son of the Father ('Fine-tuning' and 'An ever-flowing river'). Finally, we unearth a *fourth layer* when we see that our prayer actually consists in being introduced into Jesus' own prayer ('A room not of our making').

Let us begin therefore with the first layer: Jesus teaches us to pray.

Only two Gospels narrate the teaching of the *Our Father* to the disciples: Matthew and Luke.[1] The defining feature of Luke's version is that this happens when Jesus himself is praying. The passage starts with this sentence: *One day Jesus was praying in a certain place.*[2] This time he was not praying alone and in a solitary place[3] as usual, but where he could be seen by his disciples.

Of course Jesus valued the intimate character of personal prayer. He insisted that its proper place is not where one can be seen by others, but in one's room, behind a closed door, in secret.[4] Whenever he prayed, he would choose desert places or mountains, often early in the morning, when everyone else was still asleep. Not because there is anything to hide in praying, or anything to be ashamed of, but to preserve its freedom, to make sure that our motives are pure, that we engage in it truly out of love for the Father, and because we value our relationship with the Father

[1] Mt. 6.5–14 and Lk. 11.1–13.
[2] Lk. 11.1.
[3] Cf. Mt. 14.23 and Mk. 1.35.
[4] Mt. 6.5–6.

above all else. We do not pray *to be seen by other people*[5] and to give us an aura of spirituality that increases our reputation or our power over others. We pray because we need this relationship with the Father.

Thus, if this time Jesus prays in a place where his disciples can see him it is because the moment has come to teach them how to pray by drawing them into his own prayer. And sure enough the disciples are puzzled and fascinated by this sight: how long he stayed there, motionless, his eyes closed, intent on something that absorbed him utterly: it seemed as though he might carry on for hours. Something mysterious, something valuable was happening and, however perplexed by it, none of the disciples dared to interrupt Jesus – despite their impatience, none of them went to him until he had ceased to pray. Not that Jesus would have rebuked them – he loved them, and had any of them approached Jesus when he was praying, he would just have opened his eyes, smiled, and listened to him. Prayer needs quiet to thrive but the test of its authenticity is that noise and disruption do not bother it, but can be welcomed with the peace, kindness and gentleness that are the

[5] Mt. 6.5.

unmistakeable signs of the presence and action of the Holy Spirit.[6]

The disciples were waiting. Jesus knew they were observing him but he went on praying. Letting them wait was the beginning of his teaching on prayer. It meant that the first secret of prayer is that it lasts, it needs time to sink in and search deep into our hearts. Praying is *dwelling* with the Father, *remaining in his love*.[7] We do not just need to know that we are loved, we need to feel this love, to let its warmth and its light awaken the seeds sown by the word of God in our hearts and allow them time to bear fruit.

Thus Jesus asks us to pray because he himself prays. He too needs to pray, he needs to dwell with the Father, to remain in his love just as much as we do. This is what he teaches the disciples when they finally ask him, *Lord, teach us to pray*, and he answers, *'When you pray, say: Father!'*[8]

---

[6] Gal. 5.22–25.
[7] Jn 15.10.
[8] Lk. 11.1ff.

UNEXPECTED GLIMPSES

Here we reach our second layer: the way Jesus teaches us to pray corresponds to how he himself prays. Jesus too uses the *Our Father* in his prayer. Hints to this can be found in many pages of the Gospels, whenever we are afforded glimpses into Jesus' own prayer.

Some of these glimpses are sudden and unexpected. They are like geysers that suddenly burst into the open air because groundwater has come into contact with hot rocks. They express a joy that Jesus cannot contain any more: *At that time, full of joy through the Holy Spirit, Jesus said: 'I praise you, Father . . .'*[1] Glimpses like this are not meant to teach us how to pray, they simply tell us what happens when Jesus prays. When Jesus prays he does exactly what he teaches us: he calls God *Father*.

'No big deal', we might be tempted to think, and yet it is this that makes the whole difference, it is this that makes the *Our Father* not just one prayer among

[1] Lk. 10.21; cf. Mt. 11.25.

many, but *the* prayer. We can say *Father* only because Jesus says it himself. The possibility of calling God *Father* not only as Jesus does, but with him, is the gift of the risen Christ, the result of his death and his resurrection. Only after he has risen from the dead does Jesus' Father become *our* Father, as we learn from his sentence to Mary Magdalene: *I am returning to my Father and your Father.*[2]

Interestingly, the glimpse into the content of Jesus' prayer quoted above corresponds to the initial sentence of the *Our Father*. When Jesus is saying, *I praise you Father,*[3] is he not *hallowing the Father's name?* This is what he does elsewhere for example when he expands the sentence *your will be done on earth as it is in heaven,* affirming that it is the Father's *good pleasure* to hide things from the wise and learned and reveal them to little children.[4] Or again elsewhere, he expands the sentence *Your kingdom come* when he acknowledges that everything belongs to the Father, everything comes from the Father, that the work he has come to accomplish is the Father's: *All things have been committed to me by my Father.*[5]

[2] Jn 20.17.
[3] Mt. 11.25.
[4] Mt. 11.25.
[5] Mt. 11.27.

This means that the *Our Father* is first of all Jesus' own prayer, and this is confirmed by another interesting finding in the Gospels. In some rare but crucial moments of Jesus' life, we are offered glimpses not only of his prayer to the Father but also of the Father's answer. We are actually told what the Father tells Jesus when he prays:

> Now when all the people were baptized, and when Jesus also had been baptized and was praying, the heaven was opened, and the Holy Spirit descended upon him in bodily form like a dove. And a voice came from heaven, 'You are my Son, the Beloved; with you I am well pleased.'[6]

In the Gospels of Mark and Matthew we hear the Father's voice both at the baptism and at the transfiguration, but it is addressed to the people who surrounded Jesus during those events: *This is my Son, the Beloved; with him I am well pleased; listen to him!*[7] In contrast, in the version of the baptism by Luke just quoted we are told that Jesus at that moment was praying and therefore the Father's sentence is addressed to him *You are my Son . . . with you I am well*

[6] Lk. 3.21–22.
[7] Mt. 17.5; cf. also Mk 9.7; Lk. 9.35.

pleased.[8] And as this happens, the Holy Spirit descends upon him in the form of a dove.

After the decision of Adam and Eve to go their own way, to be like God, to decide by themselves what is good and what is evil, they had been driven out of the garden of Eden, a cherubim had been placed at its door and *a sword flaming and whirling guarded the way to the tree of life.*[9] This is reversed at Jesus' baptism: heaven, the way to Eden – that is, the possibility of re-establishing a loving relation with God – was restored. This is signified by *the Holy Spirit descending in bodily form like a dove*: communication between heaven and earth was re-established, because this is what the Holy Spirit is. He is the link, the communication, the connection between the Father and the Son; he is the love they have for each other, that which unites them, the life they constantly exchange.

When Jesus says *All things have been handed over to me by my Father; and no one knows the Son except the Father, and no one knows the Father except the Son and anyone to whom the Son chooses to reveal him,*[10] he is talking of the Holy Spirit, that which the Father hands down to the Son

[8] Cf. also Mk 1.11 where the Father's sentence is addressed to Jesus as well, although it is not said that he was praying as in Luke's Gospel.
[9] Gen. 3.24.
[10] Mt. 11.27ff.

and the Son gives back in thankfulness to the Father: at that time Jesus said, 'I thank you, Father . . .'[11] Thanks to the Holy Spirit the Father knows the Son and the Son knows the Father and through the Holy Spirit we too are introduced into their reciprocal knowledge, which is also and inseparably their reciprocal love. All that Jesus does, and especially his prayer, always happens 'in the Holy Spirit', as in the sentence quoted above: *At that time, full of joy through the Holy Spirit, Jesus said: 'I praise you, Father . . .'*[12]

These glimpses into Jesus' prayer so far teach us that when he prays Jesus too says the *Our Father*: he calls *Father*, the Father answers *my Son*, and in that moment the Spirit descends on him. Jesus, of course, says many other things to his Father. But all he says can be summed up in this vocative and in the trust, the familiarity, the intimacy it conveys. And all the Father says to Jesus can be summed up in these words and their corollary: 'My Son, I love you and I am pleased with you, and I show my love for you by pouring out my Holy Spirit on you, by pouring my love into your heart.'[13]

[11] Mt. 11.25ff.
[12] Lk. 10.21.
[13] Cf. Rom. 5.5: 'God's love has been poured into our hearts through the Holy Spirit that has been given to us.'

FINE-TUNING

We reach here the third layer in our exploration of the *Our Father*, namely that it is not just what Jesus *says* to the Father, but that it expresses what it means for Jesus *to be* the Son of the Father. Here we find the decisive answer to the question of why Jesus prays. Let us think about this paradox for a moment: Jesus is God. As God's Son he is always united with the Father. Does he really need to hear the Father telling him: *You are my Son?* Is he not aware of this already? Does he somehow forget it?

In our search for an answer to this question we have to rule out one possible and tempting explanation, namely that Jesus prays just to set us an example we can imitate, merely to teach us *how* to pray. This explanation has its part of truth, but is not the real answer to our question. In fact, Jesus prays not only when the disciples see him or when he is about to teach them how to pray or indeed when he wants to introduce us into his own prayer. Jesus prays all the time!

Jesus prays early in the morning, before anyone, including his disciples, is awake: *In the morning, while it was still very dark, he got up and went out to a deserted place, and there he prayed.*[1] He prays after the multiplication of the loaves: *And after he had dismissed the crowds, he went up the mountain by himself to pray.*[2] He prays before the revelation of his true identity to his disciples: *Once when Jesus was praying alone, with only the disciples near him, he asked them, 'Who do the crowds say that I am?'*;[3] before choosing his apostles: *Now during those days he went out to the mountain to pray; and he spent the night in prayer to God;*[4] in the middle of his ministry, after he has preached: *But now more than ever the word about Jesus spread abroad; many crowds would gather to hear him and to be cured of their diseases. But he would withdraw to deserted places and pray.*[5] Finally, he prays at Gethsemane, before the beginning of his passion: *They went to a place called Gethsemane; and he said to his disciples, 'Sit here while I pray.'*[6]

Prayer is a feature of his life, something he does because he needs it – and this can be a bit of a mystery

[1] Mk 1.35.
[2] Mt. 14.23.
[3] Lk. 9.18.
[4] Lk. 6.12.
[5] Lk. 5.15f.
[6] Mk 14.32.

for us: how is it possible that God needs to pray? We need to pray to God, but how can God need to pray to God?

The answer to this question lies in the content of Jesus' prayer that we explored earlier. We saw that the Father says more than once to Jesus: '*You are my Son, the Beloved; with you I am well pleased.*'[7] Here the Father is not talking to the people surrounding Jesus; he is addressing him directly. It is as if, at the decisive moments of his life, Jesus needed to hear from the Father the words, *You are my Son.* This is what the Father says to Jesus each time he prays because this is Jesus' fundamental mission: to be Son, to act as Son not only in his eternal existence in the bosom of the Father but also as one of us, as a human being like us, in our wounded flesh, with our weak wills, our muddled minds, our shaky hearts and, yes, even with our sin.

At moments of crisis in Jesus' life the focus of the temptation he undergoes tends to be strikingly similar. We see this at its most dramatic in the desert, where two out of three of the devil's attempts to win Jesus over are introduced by the same words: *'If you*

[7] Mk 1.10-11 and Lk. 3.21-22.

are the Son of God, command these stones to become loaves of bread . . . If you are the Son of God, throw yourself down.'[8] The temptations focus on what it means to be the Son of God. The devil suggests to Jesus that sonship is defined by the free use of the power that goes with it: he who was going to multiply bread for five thousand people could easily turn stones into bread; he who would later walk on water could easily fly if he wanted: he was God!

This is how the devil would have behaved had he been God and in all likelihood it is how we would behave if we were God and had this power. To be really God, however, to be the Son of the Father whom Jesus reveals to us, is something entirely different, something which the whole of Jesus' life, teaching and ministry is meant to make manifest to us – more, to make possible for us to live on a human level.

Jesus is not in the desert, in this place of temptation, by accident or because he has got lost on his way from the Jordan to wherever he was heading. The Gospel is positive about this: *Jesus was led up into the wilderness by the Spirit.*[9] He was led into this trial by the Spirit. He was there to do whatever the Father had intended him

[8] Mt. 4.1–7.
[9] Mt. 4.1.

66

to do and was determined to follow the Father's guidance, to go only where the Spirit led him, to do only what the Spirit told him to do, just as the people of Israel in the desert would only move when the cloud moved and would follow where it led.[10]

Just as the sin of our first parents had been that of mistrusting their creator and Father and thus disobeying him, so the salvation Jesus was to realize had to take the form of complete trust and obedience, because we can only obey where and when we fully trust the person leading us. The people in the desert murmured because they did not trust God: they whined when they were thirsty, complained when they were hungry, grumbled when they felt trapped with the sea in front of them and the Egyptian army behind, just like us. As soon as something happens in our life that threatens us, as soon as we are in need or in a difficult situation, we are tempted to doubt God's presence, God's providence; we find it hard to believe that he will not let us down.

To be sons of the Father, to act like sons, to trust and obey like sons, is something that does not come naturally to us, it is a constant battle that we never

[10] Exod. 40.36.

win once and for all. It is a great consolation therefore to know that it was a battle for Jesus too, that he too had to learn this lesson, he too had to feel how hard it can be at times.

Here we find the heart of the matter: for the way Jesus fought this battle, the way he learnt how to be the Son, the way he constantly 'fine-tuned' his sonship to his Father's love, was through *prayer*.

Jesus needed prayer because when he prayed he heard the Father telling him, reminding him, assuring him: *You are my Son. You are my beloved. I love you.* Jesus needed to hear this, not only once at the baptism and another time at the transfiguration just before his passion. He needed to hear this all the time, every day, every morning when he woke. When it was still dark, his first concern was this: to fine-tune his will to his Father's will, to call him *Abba! Father!* and to be told *You are my Son*; to position himself in the right way in relation to his Father. The *Our Father* is not just a prayer among others, it enshrines the *posture* we have to adopt in the Father's presence.

AN EVER-FLOWING RIVER

It is intriguing to see that whenever Jesus has enjoyed a sensational success, drawing large crowds by his preaching and miracles, he withdraws to a solitary place to pray: *In the morning, while it was still very dark, he got up and went out to a deserted place, and there he prayed.* This puzzles his disciples: *Simon and his companions hunted for him.* When they found him, they said to him, '*Everyone is searching for you.*' *He answered, 'Let us go on to the neighbouring towns, so that I may proclaim the message there also; for that is what I came out to do.' And he went throughout Galilee, proclaiming the message in their synagogues and casting out demons.*[1]

The contrast between the attitude of Jesus and that of the disciples is telling: they take this success at its face value, they do not have the reflex to check it against the Father's will, to see if this is the way the coming of the kingdom is advanced, the Father's name hallowed. And this is understandable since Jesus still has to teach them these things. Jesus, on the contrary,

[1] Mk 1.35–39.

prays and in this prayer steps back from the events, does not let the events determine his response. He wants to make sure he is doing the Father's will, he repeats *Thy will be done* . . .

The same happens after the multiplication of the loaves, if anything with even greater determination on Jesus' part, as it appears in particular in John's version of this miracle: *When Jesus realized that they were about to come and take him by force to make him king, he withdrew again to the mountain by himself.*[2] No more distressing illustration of idolatry can be found than this attempt to take God by force and make him king, apparently submitting to him, but in reality putting him at our disposal, at the disposal of our needs and whims. This can be tempting for any leader, just as it is fatal for any leader's freedom, but it is not the Son's way of being in relation to the Father. Therefore, Jesus withdraws, on the mountain, alone, in the secret of his room,[3] in the freedom of his relation to the Father, and there he can again hear the liberating and consoling *You are my Son . . . You are my Son . . .*

No surprise then to see that Jesus also prays at the moment of Peter's confession, when the Father

[2] Jn 6.15.
[3] Cf. Mt. 6.6.

reveals Jesus' real identity. Just before this, Jesus again withdraws to pray, feeling the need to ensure that he is wholly attuned to what the Father is about to reveal concerning his identity as Son, and as God. *Once when Jesus was praying alone, with only the disciples near him, he asked them, 'Who do the crowds say that I am?'*[4] That moment of prayer revealed itself as critical when Peter, just after confessing Jesus' true identity, became the mouthpiece of Satan and voiced the greatest of all temptations against Jesus:

> From that time on, Jesus began to show his disciples that he must go to Jerusalem and undergo great suffering at the hands of the elders and chief priests and scribes, and be killed, and on the third day be raised. And Peter took him aside and began to rebuke him, saying, 'God forbid it, Lord! This must never happen to you.' But he turned and said to Peter, 'Get behind me, Satan! You are a stumbling-block to me; for you are setting your mind not on divine things but on human things.'[5]

Had Jesus not been prepared for this, had he not had his mind fixed on divine things, had he not, thanks

[4] Lk. 9.18.
[5] Mt. 16.21–25.

to his prayer, made sure of being in the right posture with regard to the Father, this temptation, all the more unexpected and confusing because it came from the very person who one minute before had been the instrument of the Father's revelation, this temptation could have been fatal to him.

Finally, and most importantly, Jesus prays at Gethsemane, before the beginning of his passion, when he needs more than ever to unite his will to the Father's: *He said, 'Abba, Father, for you all things are possible; remove this cup from me; yet, not what I want, but what you want.'*[6] Through this prayer he would find the strength to be faithful until the end, to persevere even when the temptation to doubt the Father's love and faithfulness becomes unbearable.

These instances leave no room for doubt: Jesus prays because *he needs to*. What is at stake in Jesus' prayer is his very identity and his mission. Jesus does not pray *despite* the fact that he is God, as a concession to the human condition he has taken through the Incarnation. Jesus prays *because* he is God. Prayer is the highest and most telling embodiment of what it means to be God, of what it is to be the Son of God.

[6] Mk 14.36.

To be Son, to act as the Son, is something Jesus never takes for granted, never considers as understood once for all, as fulfilled once for all. He needs to learn continually what it is to be Son, how to act as Son, by hearing the Father telling him as often as possible: *You are my Son.* This entails no diminution of the divinity of the Son because *this is what to be Son is*. Not only in his earthly life but already in the eternal life of the Trinity, to be Son is never something received from the Father once for all but has to happen all the time, just as a river has to keep flowing, and a spring gushing. The Father is continually engaged in pouring out his life, his love and his Spirit on the Son. Even in the eternal life of the Trinity the Father is continually saying, *You are my Son.* And the Son exists as Son precisely by continually receiving this life, this love and this Spirit from the Father and giving them back to him. Jesus' prayer is the human 'translation', so to speak, of his eternal relation with the Father.

To be Son, to be Father, even in the middle of the life of the Trinity, is *a relationship*, something continually happening, yet ever new. Like the river we have just mentioned, it has to keep flowing. The moment it stops flowing the river ceases to exist. Prayer is at the heart of Jesus' life because it shapes his identity, it feeds his relation to the Father, it keeps the love flowing in, this love he receives from the Father and gives back to him, the love that is the Holy Spirit.

In his human life, in his decisions, in his temptations, in all the decisive moments of his ministry, Jesus feels the need to *see what the Father is doing; for whatever the Father does, the Son does likewise.*[7] He needs to make sure that the needle of his compass keeps pointing to the Father, that all he does is for the Father's glory. He needs to hear the Father confirming this to him by saying *I am pleased with what you are doing.*

Thus, when Jesus teaches us how to pray, it is his relationship with the Father that he is revealing to us. His long prayer in John's Gospel tells us as much:

> I ask that they may all be one. As you Father are in me and I am in you, may they also be in us. I in them and you in me, that they may become completely one. I know you Father and I made your name known to them so that the love with which you have loved me may be in them, and I in them.[8]

[7] Jn 5.19.
[8] Jn 17.21, 23, 25.

Indeed, the love the Father gives to the Son, that is the Holy Spirit, is that which the Son gives to us. The glory the Son receives from the Father, that is, his Sonship, is what he shares with us in making us sons in the Son. And since we are sons in the Son, we now know the *name* of the Father, we can sanctify his name, *Hallowed be thy name*, with our lips and with our life, by learning more and more how to be and live and act like children of God, by praying like children of God, by saying *Our Father*.

A ROOM NOT OF OUR MAKING

Our journey through Jesus' prayer has, hopefully, shed a new and brighter light on what was said earlier about the *Our Father* not being a prayer, nor Jesus just giving us some words, some nicely put formulas, some fitting or effective ways of addressing God. In the *Our Father* we are given not *a prayer*, but *a posture*, we are plugged into Jesus' own way of positioning himself in relation to the Father. The *Our Father* enshrines and expresses who Jesus really is, what it means that he is Son of the Father and what it means for us to become, through him, children of the Father and sons of God by being united to the only Son, Jesus himself.

We reach here the fourth layer in our journey into Christian prayer and discover that through the *Our Father* we are introduced into Jesus' own prayer.

Let us go back to the sentence in Luke's Gospel where Jesus teaches us how to pray: 'He was praying in a certain place, and after he had finished, one of his disciples said to him, "Lord, teach us to pray, as John taught his disciples." He said to them, "When you pray, say this . . ."'[1] As we noticed earlier, Luke makes it clear that the disciples ask Jesus to teach them to pray precisely because *he is praying himself*. This detail opens up to us the most distinctive feature of Christian prayer, namely that *it is not our prayer*, it is prayer only and insofar as we let ourselves be introduced into Jesus' own prayer and through it into his relation with the Father through the Holy Spirit.

The passage in Luke's Gospel where Jesus teaches his disciples how to pray should be read in parallel with Luke's account of the transfiguration: 'Now about eight days after these sayings Jesus took with him Peter and John and James, and went up on the mountain to pray.'[2] Matthew adds a detail here which in his Gospel has a special significance: 'Six days later, Jesus took with him Peter and James and his brother John and led them up a high mountain, by themselves.'[3] This *by themselves* is very important. The place of personal prayer is one's room or the secret, i.e. a space where each one of us can find the freedom to stay in God's presence: this idea is dear to Matthew. Thus, even though Matthew does not say that Jesus

[1] Lk. 11.1ff.
[2] Lk. 9.28.
[3] Mt. 17.1.

78

took the disciples up to the mountain to pray with them as Luke does, he suggests it by this little detail: 'by themselves' (or 'apart', *kath'idian* in Greek). It is as if Jesus was taking the disciples into his own room, that is into his own prayer, into his own relation with the Father, into his own freedom, the freedom of the Son who is able to call his father *Abba*!

Given this, it is hard to decide whether Peter's attitude during the transfiguration is touching or pathetic: 'Peter said to Jesus, "Lord, it is good for us to be here. If you wish, I will put up three shelters one for you, one for Moses and one for Elijah."'[4]

Even though Jesus tells us to go into our room to pray, we soon have to discover that this room is not of our own making; it is not a shelter where we can contain, so to speak, this experience and somehow make it ours, possess it. This room is a space that God alone can create for us, a space we find only when Jesus leads us. In whichever way we might understand the meaning of Matthew's *room* and *secret*, it is always Jesus' own room, his space and secret and freedom, and we are introduced into it only by his Spirit, the Spirit he gave us after his resurrection.

[4] Mt. 17.4.

In fact, as we also saw earlier, prayer is an impossible task, something we cannot achieve, something we are not capable of: *We do not know how to pray.*[5] But what could be a discouraging, a dispiriting truth, becomes the very reason of our consolation when we realize that the Lord comes to our help: 'I lift up my eyes to the hills: from where will my help come? My help comes from the Lord, who made heaven and earth.'[6]

The transfiguration is not the only occasion on which Jesus took Peter, Jacob and James to pray with him. There is another moment, just before his passion, when they were invited to accompany him, this time to the garden of Gethsemane: Then he said to them, 'I am deeply grieved, even to death; remain here, and stay awake with me.'[7] He said to them, 'Pray that you may not come into the time of trial.'[8] Peter, James and John, the same disciples who had seen his glory at the transfiguration are now the witnesses of his anxiety, struggle and fear.

This time Jesus explicitly begs them to stay awake with him, to pray with him, because the only hope of his coping with this decisive hour lies in the strength

[5] Rom. 8.26.
[6] Ps. 121.1–2.
[7] Mt. 26.38.
[8] Lk. 22.40.

80

that the Father alone can give. And we know the story: the disciples fell asleep! In this decisive moment, *we* all fall asleep:

> Then he came to the disciples and found them sleeping; and he said to Peter, 'So, could you not stay awake with me one hour? Stay awake and pray that you may not come into the time of trial; the spirit indeed is willing, but the flesh is weak.' . . . Then he came to the disciples and said to them, 'Are you still sleeping and taking your rest? See, the hour is at hand, and the Son of Man is betrayed into the hands of sinners.'[9]

Mark adds that *their eyes were very heavy; and they did not know what to say to him.*[10] Luke attributes this sleep to grief: 'When he got up from prayer, he came to the disciples and found them sleeping because of grief, and he said to them, "Why are you sleeping? Get up and pray that you may not come into the time of trial."'[11]

But this incapacity to pray, to stay awake with Jesus, is just as overpowering at the transfiguration. In Mark's

[9] Mt. 26.40, 41, 45.
[10] Mk 14.40.
[11] Lk. 22.45f.

Gospel Peter does not know what to say;[12] in Luke's version, Peter and his companions were weighed down with sleep.[13] What more telling illustration of Paul's humble acknowledgment: indeed, *We do not know how to pray*.[14] We are left powerless when we are introduced into Jesus' space, into his room, into his secret, into his relation with the Father. The cloud is so bright, the light is so dazzling, that we are blinded.

This is why being taught how to pray is not enough. Even to be taken by Jesus to pray *with* him (as at the transfiguration and in the garden of Gethsemane) is not enough. Our only chance of praying is being introduced *into* Jesus' own prayer, being one with him, letting him pray in us through his Spirit. Indeed, this is what the *Our Father* is really about: not simply being taught how to pray, but being introduced into Jesus' prayer.

When it comes to prayer, *unless the Lord builds the house, those who build it labour in vain*.[15] No space is more in need of being built by the Lord than the space of prayer, than the inner and outer atmosphere where we can pray, than the room behind the door of which

[12] Mk 9.6.
[13] Lk. 9.32.
[14] Rom. 8.26.
[15] Ps. 127.1.

we are commanded to withdraw. Certainly, there are places more conducive to prayer than others, but the best environment in the world can prove empty and useless for prayer unless we are led by Jesus into the right space, into the right room, into the right *posture* – which is nothing else than the room, the space, the posture, the cloud, the relation between him and the Father filled by the Holy Spirit.

We now understand what happens, then, when we say the *Our Father*. It is a prayer that cannot just stay on our lips but somehow takes us into a special 'place' right in the heart of divine life. It is something like what happens when we are invited to lunch by a family. We do not just sit at their table and take some food but we are embraced by that family, we have a share in the joy, the love, the warmth of the relations between husband, wife and children.

Similarly, when we pray, we sit at the table of the Trinity: the Father, the Son and the Holy Spirit – we have a share in the joy and the love that they exchange with each other, we become part of the family of God. A more 'theological' way of stating the same truth is this: when we say the *Our Father* we are united with Jesus, because the Spirit says *Abba Father* in our hearts and the Father sees in our faces the face of his beloved Son.

This is what Jesus promises to us: *As you, Father, are in me and I am in you, may they also be in us.*[16] This is what the expression *Our Father* means: 'You whom we can call Father because you are *Jesus' Father* and we are one with Jesus.' This is what was revealed by Jesus himself when he said to Mary Magdalene: *Do not hold on to me, because I have not yet ascended to the Father. But go to my brothers and say to them, 'I am ascending to my Father and your Father, to my God and your God.'*[17] With Jesus' resurrection his Father became our Father, because then he sent the Spirit in our hearts – and we know that in our heart he cries *Abba Father*!

Thus, the space of prayer, the room we have to go into, is the life of the Trinity, the relation between the Son with the Father and the Father with the Son through the Holy Spirit. Until we have understood this point, the Trinity remains a distant and abstract mystery, with no bearing on our spiritual life, on our prayer, on our Christian identity. The Trinity can be understood and presented as an explanation of what it takes for God to make us pray, of what prayer is, of how to pray, of what happens when we pray!

[16] Jn 17.21.
[17] Jn 20.17.

84

THE RIGHT POSTURE

In our search for the secret of prayer we have been led into the inner life of God, or what theology calls the mystery of the Trinity. We might wonder if this is not taking things a bit too far. We want to learn how to pray and we are given abstract theological ideas instead. What does this mean in practice? How can it truly help us to pray?

The main insight we have gained so far is that before being a question of method, environment and place, the secret of prayer lies in finding the right *posture*. Advice on prayer often starts with the external posture – how to sit or kneel, how to breathe – before passing to inner dispositions and the need to cultivate calm peace, patience and perseverance. All these elements merit attention and can be very helpful, especially at the beginning of the life of prayer, but they are still not the *posture* which is required by prayer or, rather, the posture that is prayer.

When, for instance, I want to write a letter on a sensitive point to a dear friend I need to sit down, grab my laptop and make sure I have a nice mug of coffee close at hand – more pertinently, I might have to switch off my iPhone and try to focus on what I need to tell the person I love. But is this enough? Is this the key to finding the right words? Is it all I need to do? Writing to a dear friend requires something more. I have to connect with that part of myself where my friend matters, where the treasure of all I have shared with him is jealously kept, where I can find the inspiration I need. I have to find the right 'place', the right inner disposition, because only what comes from there will sound heartfelt and sincere.

Prayer likewise can be heartfelt and sincere only when it stems from the right place, only when we embark on it with the right posture. We have looked at Jesus' posture in prayer. We have also seen that Jesus' prayer is the one authentic prayer, the same that is continually active in our hearts whether we are aware of it or not, the prayer of the Holy Spirit. When Jesus prays he says *Father!* In the same way, the Spirit of the Son cries in our hearts: *Abba, Father!*[1] We know therefore that this inner attitude resembles the way

[1] Gal. 4.6.

children look at their fathers; that is, with trust, affection, gratitude and a desire to please – at least if our experience of earthly fatherhood has been a positive one, something which unfortunately cannot be taken for granted.

I once met a Christian woman from the Far East who was traumatized by the idea of addressing God as father. Her own father had been cold and distant, and a relationship with him had been impossible. This aspect of her faith had left her resentful and even angry. In time, however, she turned this anger, not against herself, but against the cold and distant projection of God determined by her experience of fatherhood, whereupon the mirror broke into pieces and she discovered the real Father, a Father who loved and cared for her. The *Our Father* became real for her and this led to the healing of her relationship with her own earthly father before he died.

We often think that to be a father and to be a son or daughter should come spontaneously to us, but then the more we grow, the more we discover not only all we owe to our parents, but also all the ways in which they have conditioned and hurt us. At that moment we need to start learning what it means to be sons or daughters (and indeed fathers or mothers) in a new and different way. With our Father in heaven we go through a similar process. We become children of God through baptism, but then it takes the whole of our life on earth to realize it and act like children of this Father, to think, pray, forgive, love and rest like children of our Father, God.

The whole of Jesus' life, teaching and miracles can be seen in this light: he shows to us what it is to be children of the Father, he teaches us how to grow into this posture, he heals the blindness, the deafness, the paralysis, the fear and all that prevents us from saying and living out the *Our Father* authentically. And if we look for the most inspiring pages of the New Testament on this point, Christian tradition and spirituality point us to Jesus' sermon on the mount, in chapters 5–7 of Matthew's Gospel, often referred to as the *Magna Carta* of the Christian life.

This is a finely chiselled text. It captures what lies at the heart of Christian life. It explains what being a Christian really means, i.e. how Christians should and can be the salt of the earth and the light of the world. The core of the message enshrined in this sermon is located in the teaching on Christian justice and perfection conveyed in the following sentences: 'Strive first for the kingdom of God and his righteousness, and all these things will be given to you as well.'[2] 'Be perfect, therefore, as your heavenly Father is perfect.'[3]

But there remains another layer to peel off before the essence of the teaching is revealed: we have to ask ourselves: what is the *justice* Jesus wants us to seek first? What is the *perfection* we have to live in relation to the Father? It is summed up in one phrase slipped into Jesus' teaching, a few words that might easily go unnoticed: *so that you may be children of your Father in heaven*.[4]

Not children in a general way. Not simply loyal sons or daughters of any good father and mother on this earth, but children 'of *your* Father in heaven', of this Father, of *my* Father, namely Jesus' Father. This is the righteousness of the Gospel, the perfection of Christian life: to act as real children of this Father, *so that you may be children of your Father in heaven*. And we already know that the only way to be children of this Father is to be one with his only child, his only Son who alone totally pleases him, who alone is perfect, Jesus, the only person to whom the Father can say: *You are my Son, the Beloved; with you I am well pleased.*[5]

[2] Mt. 6.33.
[3] Mt. 5.48.
[4] Mt. 5.45.
[5] Lk. 3.22.

The sermon on the mount describes what we have called Jesus' *posture* in his relation to the Father, in his prayer, and therefore the *posture* which all authentic children of this Father need to adopt.

This description is well known: the children of the Father are poor in spirit, are meek, they thirst for justice, they are merciful, pure in heart, peace-makers and often suffer for the cause of justice. They go beyond the letter of the law in the sense that they are not satisfied with abstaining from evil acts, but try to avoid complicity with evil in their hearts, above all when it comes to forgiving their enemies. They also go beyond what is required by almsgiving, prayer and fasting, by making sure they put their heart into it. In so doing they develop new eyes and a new heart.

Of course these words are as beautiful as they are daunting – and vice versa. It is not an accident if several of the vivid images of this sermon have, in our different cultures, become synonymous with the excessive or indeed the impossible: turning the other cheek instead of retaliating, gouging out our eye to avoid committing adultery, minding the plank in our own eye instead of obsessing about the speck in our neighbour's – the list could go on for a while.

For all its beauty, this sermon tends to be seen as rather discouraging. Who among us can reach such a level of purity, forgiveness, generosity, selflessness, coherence? Mercifully, there is another way of tackling these pages, a way which does not read them simply as a moral code of conduct, but first and foremost as a portrait of Jesus: of his justice, his perfection, his purity, his forgiveness. They explain why the Father is well pleased with him.[6] Only because and insofar as we are united with him do they apply to us too. And this is something that before being *striven for* has to be asked for, *prayed for*.

In fact, the whole of this sermon can be seen as a chest for one invaluable pearl, Jesus' most priceless gift to us. Indeed, where do we find the *Our Father* in Matthew's Gospel? Here, right in the middle of this sermon, as the key to its meaning and as the only way in which its impossible standard can make sense for us too. In the sermon on the mount everything we are called to become and do becomes the object of prayer; everything we are called to become and to do is to be desired, waited for and welcomed as a gift. Prayer thus becomes *the long and persevering patience through which we become children of God*.

[6] Lk. 3.22.

Becoming children of this Father, of our Father in heaven, is something we have to pray for with patience: 'Ask, and it will be given to you; search, and you will find; knock, and the door will be opened for you. For everyone who asks receives, and everyone who searches finds, and for everyone who knocks, the door will be opened.'[7] Here Jesus teaches us that patience does not mean passivity. Prayer entails an active patience: we are called to ask, search, knock, that is pray. It is a patience that, when it receives what was prayed for, welcomes it as a gift.

Prayer as patience is the secret of the Christian life and should be the salt and the light of everything we do, for only that which is planted by the Father bears fruit, since 'every plant that my heavenly Father has not planted will be uprooted'.[8]

[7] Mt. 7.7–8.
[8] Mt. 15.13.

OVERCOMING SUSPICION

When we look for the right *posture* in prayer, when we
listen to the sermon on the mount to learn how to be
introduced into Jesus' own prayer, that is into his own
relation with the Father, we are invited not to look
at ourselves but at him. Spiritual tradition is unani-
mous on this point: Christian life consists in striving
to keep our eyes fixed on Jesus.[1] We must *forget what
is behind and strain towards what is ahead, press on to take
hold of that for which Christ Jesus took hold of us.*[2]

Thus, when we hear *Blessed are the poor in spirit for theirs
is the kingdom of heaven*[3] it is to Jesus we have to turn if
we want to see what this means. This kingdom is Jesus
himself, not only what he does, but what he *is*; this kingdom is the Father's intervention in the history of the
world, in the history of my life, to change it once and
for all, through Christ, and it is this that we pray for in
the *Our Father*, when we say the words *Your kingdom come*.

[1] Heb. 12.2.
[2] Phil. 3.12–13.
[3] Mt. 5.3.

93

The kingdom of God becomes *ours*, i.e. we correspond to God's decisive intervention in history by being *poor in spirit*. 'Poverty' here does not mean 'destitution'. More than a condition it is an awareness; this is why it is called poverty *of spirit*. It is the deep, trusting, joyful awareness of our total dependence on God. Not a grudging addiction to someone who takes advantage of this to diminish, enslave and humiliate us, but the grateful reliance on a Father who gives us everything and desires nothing in return other than our fulfilment, by which he is glorified. It is the grateful familiarity Adam and Eve experienced when God went to stroll with them in the cool of the evening just to enjoy their company and rejoice in their wonder at all the beauty of the creation with which he had surrounded them.

What a wonderful *posture* this is for our prayer! Poverty of spirit, the awareness of our dependence on God, the reliance on his love for us, the experience of his familiarity, the wonderment at all he has given us. The more we grow into this poverty of spirit, the more we become children of God. And prayer is necessary here because this dependence, this reliance on the Father, do not come naturally to us any more. The serpent instilled in us a radical doubt about God's good intentions, he damaged our trust in the Father and left us with the idol of a god who created us only to enjoy his superiority over us, while secretly afraid of us: 'God knows that when you eat of it your eyes will be opened, and you will be like God, knowing good and evil.'[4] However much we might trust God, however much we may have experienced his love in our lives, this doubt lurks in our hearts and raises its poisonous tail whenever we face trials, difficulties and setbacks, whenever we journey through a godless desert.

Just as he did in the garden, the serpent speaks to us in these deserts; once again he insinuates doubt in our heart and persuades us to put God to the test. This is why the desert is so expedient a place for prayer. Not because of its peace and its silence, but because it confronts us with this persistent inner voice that keeps hissing its suspicion and distrust. The desert is expedient for prayer because there our idolatry cannot remain hidden any longer, and if we do not want to yield to it the only weapon at our disposal is recourse to the Father – calling patiently, doggedly: *Our Father, your glory, not my glory; your kingdom, not my kingdom; your will, not my will.*

[4] Gen. 3.5.

The desert nurtures prayer because it unmasks what lies in our heart, but also because there we learn that the Father does indeed take care of us:

> Remember the long way that the Lord your God has led you these forty years in the wilderness, in order to humble you, testing you to know what was in your heart . . . He humbled you by letting you hunger, then by feeding you with manna, with which neither you nor your ancestors were acquainted, in order to make you understand that one does not live by bread alone, but by every word that comes from the mouth of the Lord. The clothes on your back did not wear out and your feet did not swell these forty years.[5]

Prayer, like the time spent by the people of Israel in the desert, is the time, the place, the space where we are humbled, where we are shown what is in our hearts, and where we are also fed so that we can learn, little by little, that we do not live by bread alone, but by every word that comes from the mouth of the Lord. In this desert we are taught the right posture in our relation with the Father. It is Jesus who teaches it to us. We are not alone in this desert because he went there ahead of us and opened up a way for us;

[5] Deut. 8.2–4.

he forced the serpent to spit out its venom and gave us the antidote.

By teaching us the *Our Father*, Jesus prevents us from falling into the trap of the devil's twisted understanding of sonship and introduces us into his own loving, trusting, open relationship with the Father. Praying the *Our Father* in this way we learn to be *poor in spirit* and we discover the happiness, the blessing attached to it: *Blessed are the poor in spirit!* When we pray the *Our Father* in this way, in Jesus' wake, then *the kingdom of God is ours*, that is, we actively and effectively contribute to the hallowing of the Father's name, to the coming of his kingdom and to the fulfilment of his will, *on earth as it is in heaven*.

Prayer stemming from this posture, from poverty of spirit, is the kind of worship *the Father seeks*,[6] the only worship that pleases him, the worship in spirit and truth that Jesus came to inaugurate on earth.[7] It is the worship we have access to once Jesus has driven the serpent away: *Away from me, Satan! For it is written: 'Worship the Lord your God, and serve him only.'*[8] We want our prayer to grow into this worship. We want our worship to be free.

[6] Jn 4.23.
[7] Jn 4.24.
[8] Mt. 4.10.

A LARGER PICTURE

Christian spirituality still is permeated by Stoicism. God's will weighs on us as the ominous unknown factor of our lives. We are vaguely aware that our existence is ultimately determined by someone we call 'god', and we keep our fingers crossed, hoping he will not send us something unpleasant. And should he, there would be no resisting; our only option would be to bow our head in resignation. Most of the time we allow our whims, passions, circumstances and ingrained habits to lead us, and we either prefer not to think how these relate to God's will or we become very good at persuading ourselves that they *are* God's will.

It gets worse when we take God's will seriously or fancy we are doing so. We start negotiating with whatever our imagination pictures as 'god', we think that if we offer a sop to this idol, we might get what we want or need in return. When we call to mind the people who are dearest to us, the friends, the family members we do not want to lose, or when we think about things we really want, we are possessed by a vague, permanent, unspoken anxiety and we discover we are no different from any of our ancestors: we look for ways of winning over this divinity, we plunge with torches into caves, paint elaborate pictures on the walls – our dreams of happiness, our hopes, our desires, our vision of life – and leave again cautiously, sealing the entrance behind us. This should keep the divinity busy; it might like these pictures and favour us or at least leave us in peace, undisturbed.

Jesus does not pray in caves. At the strategic moments of his life he climbs mountains. Not that the Father is more available on mountains than elsewhere: *You will worship the Father neither on this mountain nor in Jerusalem.*[1] But instead of descending into the caves of anxiety, filled with human representations of the divine, Jesus rises above them, above the whirlwind of events, above anxieties and fears, to a place where he can get a larger picture. The mountains of Palestine are no higher than hills. One does not need to climb the Himalayas to pray. It is the movement that counts: not sinking but rising.

After Jesus had multiplied the loaves, people wanted to make him king, to get hold of him, to have

[1] Jn 4.21.

this wonder boy at their disposal: a provider of free food! 'When Jesus realized that they were about to come and take him by force to make him king, he withdrew again to the mountain by himself.'[2]

The disciples are excited: finally some recognition, some success; it is working, the kingdom is coming on earth. Jesus *forces them to get into the boat* and sends them *to the other side*, then hurries to dismiss this crowd of too eager worshippers. He suddenly feels the need to *go up on the mountain and pray*.[3] Prayer is the place where Jesus rises above events, above circumstances, whims, instincts, passions and temptations – the place where he reminds himself of what he really wants, of why he came.[4] If anyone ever knew why he came and what he wanted to do, it was Jesus. If anyone, ever, was determined to fulfil God's will and, furthermore, knew it, it was he. And yet he too needed to *keep awake and pray* because he, too, felt that *his spirit was willing, but his flesh was weak*.[5]

In the *Our Father* we pray: *Your will be done*. Not the will of an anonymous divinity, nor the will of one of

[2] Jn 6.15.
[3] Mk 6.45–46.
[4] Cf. Mk 1.35–38.
[5] Mk 14.38.

our many projections of God, but the will of the *Father*, of *our* Father. The Father knows what we need even before we ask him, he cares for us, he provides for us, knows the number of hairs on our head, has a project of happiness and fulfilment for each one of us. When we ask for the Father's, for *this* Father's will to be done, we are neither bowing our heads in resignation nor letting ourselves be swept away by the relentless stream of fate. Praying, on the contrary, is lifting up our eyes, meeting the Father's eyes in trust, taking our lives back from whatever threatens to influence them, reclaiming our freedom.

How can doing someone else's will be an act of freedom? Whenever I let anybody dictate from the outside what I should do, I am not free. The law makes us slaves, shackles our freedom.[6] What it enjoins me to do might be right and good, but the fact that it compels me from without is a denial of my freedom. A Christian is not under the law but is led by the Spirit: *If you are led by the Spirit, you are not subject to the law.*[7] Christians do what they do from within, because they will it, they desire it, they love it. I want the Father's will because I am his son: his

[6] Cor. 3.6.
[7] Gal. 5.18.

will is my will, my will is his will (and we say *will* and not *whims* – 'my will is his will' does not mean 'my whims are his will').

Praying consists in going to the root of our will and of our desires to discover that the Father guides us not from the outside but from within, from the 'heart' or from the 'spirit', from this place where his Spirit dwells, where he is one with our spirit, as the innermost cradle of our life, our movement, our being: *In him we live and move and have our being.*[8] Asking that *your will be done* is our highest and most effective way of reclaiming our freedom from any law, any circumstance, any person who might have authority over us in this life. We know that we are praying the words aright when *Your will be done* makes us feel free, *for freedom Christ has set us free. Stand firm, therefore, and do not submit again to a yoke of slavery.*[9]

Perhaps Jesus offers his best commentary to this sentence of the *Our Father – Your will be done –* during one of the most charming pages of the New Testament, his dialogue with the old man Nicodemus. Jesus likes Nicodemus and is not offended by the patronizing tone he adopts at the beginning of the conversation.

[8] Acts 17.28.
[9] Gal. 5.1.

A leader of the Jews, a master of the Law, an honest seeker after God, Nicodemus thinks he is open-minded. The other Pharisees have already made up their minds about Jesus, this maverick preacher from Galilee, and are set on undermining him. Nicodemus knows better: *You are a teacher who has come from God; for no one can do these signs that you do apart from the presence of God.*[10] He even takes the risk of going to speak to Jesus alone, at night.

This night is often interpreted as the symbol of his misunderstanding: he thinks he sees, but about Jesus he is in the dark. The night, however, is also the time for pondering and meditation. The leisure offered by the quiet of the night makes us more receptive – it is the best time for friendly conversations. Jesus, too, sounds relaxed, as he will be with the woman he meets at the well a while later.[11] He even becomes playful and suggests Nicodemus should consider rebirth! Nicodemus is puzzled: *How can anyone be born after having grown old? Can one enter a second time into the mother's womb and be born?*[12] He is taking Jesus too seriously . . . Why is Jesus so cryptic? Why does he not

[10] Jn 3.2.
[11] Jn 4.
[12] Jn 3.4.

reveal his identity to Nicodemus as unambiguously as he will to the woman at the well: *I am he*,[13] which means 'I am *Yahweh*?'

The answer is simple: because this is not an answer that words alone can convey, that understanding alone can welcome. One can hear the words, understand their meaning, but still not *see*. So Jesus gives Nicodemus a little lesson in epistemology, the branch of philosophy that reflects on the way we know. There are two ways of understanding things. There is the way of the *flesh* and then the way of *the spirit*: *What is born of the flesh is flesh, and what is born of the Spirit is spirit.*[14] The flesh is the symbol of the uneasy and murky mixture of whims, wishful thinking and addictions, in short of everything that hinders and reduces our freedom. We think we want something, but in reality we do not. Nicodemus thinks he wants to listen to Jesus, but he cannot even see him. He thinks he wants what God wants, but his pre-packaged idea of God, his prejudices, his condescension, all hold his will in bondage and make him the prisoner of his flesh. Once again, what comes to mind is Paul: 'I am of the flesh . . . I do not understand my own actions.

[13] Jn 4.26.
[14] Jn 3.6.

I do not do what I want, but I do the very thing I hate . . . I can will what is right, but I cannot do it. For I do not do the good I want, but the evil I do not want is what I do . . . Wretched man that I am!'[15]

Not so simple to pray *Your will be done*! Or rather, not so easy for the flesh (in Paul's sense of the word) to mean the words it utters. Any disquiet we feel when saying this prayer is an indication that it is issuing from the flesh, not the spirit. We say the words but we are unable to mean them. *No one can say 'Jesus is Lord' except by the Holy Spirit*,[16] that is, 'No one can say "Your will be done" except by the Holy Spirit.'

We need to understand better what this means.

[15] Rom. 7.14–24.
[16] Cor. 12.3.

RECLAIMING OUR FREEDOM

Your will be done. The key to the understanding of this sentence of the *Our Father* is its often-unnoticed post-script: *on earth as it is in heaven.* Yes, the prayer is not just *Your will be done,* but *Your will be done on earth as it is in heaven.*

Not any way of doing God's will is acceptable. No form of compulsion will do. Self-blackmailing will not do. Guilt will not do. Sheer willpower will not do. Duty will not do. The list is long . . . Christians specialize in parodies, caricatures and often perversions of 'doing God's will'. We can persuade ourselves that we are doing the right thing, that we are doing God's will, when in fact we are giving way to our own will instead. This is the single worst and most danger-ous form of self-delusion. We say 'your will' and we mean 'our whims', our blind, unchecked, inextrica-ble mixture of good intentions and selfish motives that spoils anything noble we hope to achieve.

The postscript *on earth as it is in heaven* is not about *what* has to be done, but about *how* it has to be done.

When we pray *Your will be done on earth as it is in heaven*, it is the 'how' we are praying for: *as it is in heaven*, i.e. as it is in the relations between the Father and the Son. Father, we want to do your will as your Son does it: spontaneously, sincerely, free from selfishness and self-delusion, free from condescension and fear, free from guilt, duty, compulsion, self-blackmailing and all such forms of bondage that have kept us in slavery for too long. Now *we have escaped like a bird from the snare of the fowlers; the snare is broken, and we have escaped.*[1]

God's will gives me the wings of a dove,[2] i.e. the freedom to act as God the Father and God the Son do, not because I have to, but because I desire to, I love to. And God's will, God's desire, God's love, have a name, they *are* the Holy Spirit. *What is born of the flesh is flesh, and what is born of the Spirit is spirit.*[3] Only if I consciously tune in with the gentle movement of the Spirit of God in my heart do I acquire a freedom that comes from within, the freedom of the Spirit – I *become* spirit. Only the wings of the Spirit deliver me

[1] Ps. 124.7.
[2] Ps. 55.6.
[3] Jn 3.6.

from the snares of everything that keeps me glued to the earth and unable to take flight.

When I pray *Your will be done as it is in heaven*, i.e. 'as it is done in the relations between the Father and the Son in the life of the Trinity', I am asking for the gift of the Holy Spirit, the love between the Father and the Son.

When I toil for hours over a translation my best friend needs for an important article he is writing, I can rely on my love for him; this love gives me an enthusiasm I would not have been able to arouse otherwise. St Augustine famously said: *Where there is love, there is no toil and even if we toil, we love this very toil.* We do whatever has to be done because we want to, we choose to – and we are not afraid of the unknown.

This is why the meaning of this prayer entirely depends on *whose* will we are talking about. Not the will of any 'god', but the will of the Father, of *our* Father. It is a commitment to a relationship, to a covenant – a commitment to a common project we love, a common life we share, a common destiny we long for.

This is why this prayer gives us wings: 'O that I had wings like a dove! I would fly away and be at rest; truly, I would flee far away; I would lodge in the wilderness; I would hurry to find a shelter for myself from the raging wind and tempest.'[4] All the Father wants is to shelter me in his bosom; all he wants, all he wills, is my freedom, my fulfilment, my life. This is the *will* I pray for when I say *Your will be done*.

This prayer also gives us eagle's wings: 'Those who wait for the Lord [those who pray] shall renew their strength, they shall mount up with wings like eagles, they shall run and not be weary, they shall walk and not faint.'[5] Again what we are promised is not conformity to an anonymous will, but a renewed agility – the spontaneity, responsiveness, alertness of love, the boldness of love: 'The wind blows where it chooses, and you hear the sound of it, but you do not know where it comes from or where it goes. So it is with everyone who is born of the Spirit.'[6]

Each time I pray *Your will be done* in my life as in the life of the Father and the Son, I am spreading the wings of my spirit, preparing to take off as soon as I feel the wind of the Spirit lift them. I know I am praying aright only if it makes me feel lighter and readier.

[4] Ps. 55.6–8.
[5] Isa. 40.31.
[6] Jn 3.8.

I know I am praying aright only if it makes *my heart* lighter and readier so that *my eyes* can see.

Heart and eyes are the first to benefit from this freedom. Jesus' remark to Nicodemus: *No one can see the kingdom of God without being born from above,*[7] means that the ability to see God depends on the new heart promised to us: 'A new heart I will give you, and a new spirit I will put within you . . . I will put my spirit within you, and make you follow my statutes and be careful to observe my ordinances.'[8]

We are promised a heart that acts not out of duty but from love. And as the heart opens, so do our eyes: *Blessed are the pure in heart, for they will see God.*[9] Our heart becomes purer in the sense that it grows into the spontaneity of desire, it wants *as* the Father wants, *on earth as it is in heaven.* And I know this is happening because my eyes begin to see things they had never noticed before.

Jesus was not only a teacher. Had teaching been enough to save us, any of the prophets would have been able to fulfil this mission. We cannot hear Jesus' teaching, because we are deaf, or see him, because

[7] Jn 3.3.
[8] Ezek. 36.26–27.
[9] Mt. 5.8.

we are blind; we cannot walk behind him, because we are paralysed and, anyway, we do not want to because our heart is hardened: 'This people's heart has grown dull, their ears are hard of hearing, they have shut their eyes so that they might not look with their eyes, and listen with their ears, and understand with their heart and turn and I would heal them.'[10]

Our heart has grown dull to the point that it has to be replaced; we need God to create a new heart for us: *Create in me a clean heart, O God, and put a new spirit within me*,[11] so that our eyes might be restored to health, and light, flooding in, dispel our inner darkness: 'The eye is the lamp of the body. So, if your eye is healthy, your whole body will be full of light; but if your eye is unhealthy, your whole body will be full of darkness. If then the light in you is darkness, how great is the darkness!'[12]

Heart and eyes always go together in Scripture, as we noticed above: *Blessed are the pure in heart, for they will see God.*[13] And purity here does not have any sexual meaning at all. Purity means openness to the Father, it

[10] Mt. 13.15.
[11] Ps. 51.10.
[12] Mt. 6.22–23.
[13] Mt. 5.8.

means adhesion to the Father's will not from without but from within. The externalized commandments have been replaced by inward dispositions: 'you shall not kill' becomes 'love your enemies'; adultery is no longer defined by outward behaviour, but by the thoughts I harbour in my heart, by the way I look at others; truth does not need the support of oaths when I mean what I say and commit to it with my heart.[14] In Jesus' teaching the 'what I do' has been replaced by 'how I do it', and if my actions are to be patterned on the life of heaven, on the relations between the Father and the Son, what I do must come from within, it has to be free, it has to be not only 'done', but chosen, loved, desired, cherished, nurtured.

The fruit of God's will, of the Father's will, only grows in the heart of a son who cherishes and nurtures the seed of the word: *The good soil is those who, when they hear the word, hold it fast in an honest and good heart, and bear fruit with perseverance.*[15] Of course there will be temptations and distractions. Of course our heart will never fully taste this freedom until the end of our lives – and this is why the aligning of our hearts in prayer with God's will is so important and has to

[14] Cf. Mt. 5.17–48.
[15] Lk. 8.15.

be renewed 'daily' – just as we need the *daily bread*, so we need the daily gift of a new heart and of a new spirit: *Create in me a clean heart, O God, and put a new spirit within me.*[16]

But this new freedom is not reserved for the life to come. Here already a taste of it can be savoured, as for example when Scripture suddenly opens up and becomes meaningful: '*Were not our hearts burning within us while he was talking to us on the road, while he was opening the scriptures to us?*'[17] Then we enjoy the blessedness of those who see: *blessed are your eyes, for they see, and your ears, for they hear.*[18] We can follow in Jesus' steps even when he walks on the water, at least for a little while:

> Peter got out of the boat, started walking on the water, and came towards Jesus. But when he noticed the strong wind, he became frightened, and beginning to sink, he cried out, 'Lord, save me!' Jesus immediately reached out his hand and caught him, saying to him, 'You of little faith, why did you doubt?'[19]

[16] Ps. 51.10.
[17] Lk. 24.32.
[18] Mt. 13.16.
[19] Mt. 14.29–31.

This freedom is ours only for as long as we keep our eyes on the Son, only as long as we *run with perseverance the race that is set before us looking to Jesus*.[20]

The freedom the Father grants us might even end up surprising us. This freedom emboldens us to the point where God's will gives way to our will, as it happened with the remarkable Syrophoenician woman who, challenged by Jesus, challenged him in return. She knew what she wanted and was ready to fight for it, even against God. She persevered, she knew how to get straight to the heart of the Father:

> She begged Jesus to cast the demon out of her daughter. He said to her, 'Let the children be fed first, for it is not fair to take the children's food and throw it to the dogs.' But she answered him, 'Sir, even the dogs under the table eat the children's crumbs.' Jesus said to her, 'For saying that, you may go – the demon has left your daughter.' So she went home, found the child lying on the bed, and the demon gone.[21]

[20] Heb. 12.1–2.
[21] Mk 7.26–30.

A NEW DAY

Pray then in this way,[1] says Jesus. Not just: 'using these words' or 'adopting this method', but 'in this freedom', in the freedom of the children of God, in the freedom of the Spirit who gives wings to our desire, who frees us from the self-absorption that prevents us from raising our eyes to God. The freedom of the Spirit that frees us from the 'me, me, me' and gives us joy and peace in repeating, 'your, your, your': *hallowed be your name, your kingdom come, your will be done*. Not in self-denial, nor by downplaying in any way our wishes, needs, hopes and desires, but by owning them in a new way, by allowing them to be purified of all dregs as we plunge in the waters of prayer.

Jesus teaches us to begin by asking that the Father's name may be *hallowed*, sanctified – and that his kingdom may come. The Father's *name* and the Father's *kingdom*: who has these at the top of his or her list of intentions in prayer? We struggle even to understand

[1] Mt. 6.9.

what either of these things mean! And yet it is so simple and so beautiful.

To take God's *name* first: God has no name, he never gives his name, he cannot give his name. When we know somebody's name – which nowadays includes the family name – we start the process of sizing him or her up, of deciding how we are going to behave with this person and of establishing boundaries. This process cannot work with God, who is free in the way Jesus tries to explain to Nicodemus: *The wind blows where it chooses, and you hear the sound of it, but you do not know where it comes from or whither it goes.*[2]

Knowing somebody, *really* knowing, only happens when my story meets the other person's story, it is a process that takes time. The more my knowledge of other people is based on a common history, the less I rely on the initial idea I had formed about them on the basis of their name because I am granted access to a deeper level of his identity – not based on how they look, on their family history, their race, gender, nationality, education, but on their character, their behaviour. Now I empathize with the other person to the point where I can anticipate the way they are going to act or react.

[2] Jn 3.8.

God has no name, nor does he give us any, not because he would feel threatened by this disclosure, but because he wants to be known by us at this deeper and authentic level. Thus, when Moses asks him his name, God's answer is *I am who I am*,[3] which means *I act in the way I act*, that is: 'If you want to know who I am pay attention to what I do for you, enter into a common history with me, join a covenant with me, and as we journey together you will understand who I really am.'

And indeed God kept Moses and the people of Israel close to him in the desert for the following forty years precisely for this reason: so that they might know him as a loving and forgiving Father who takes care of his people and wants their freedom, not only from their enslavement to the Egyptians, but even more deeply from the inner slavery to the golden calf, the ultimate idol, the false image of God, the symbol of all the projections, the screens, the walls we build between ourselves and the Father.

So God's name means *God's behaviour, God's action*, because God is what he does. Another way of saying it is that God is *Father*, God is he who has decided to father us by creating us, by strolling in friendship with

[3] Exod. 3.13–16.

us in the garden where we lived, by not abandoning us when we fled away from him to a distant country. God is Father because he fathers us not only initially, not only when he creates us. He fathers us again and in a new way by sending his only beloved Son and uniting us with him, so that now we are his children not just because he gave us life, movement and being, but also because we are loved by him and can love him in a new way, thanks to his own Spirit, whom he has poured into our hearts.

Now we can truly say that we know God's name. By teaching us how to pray, Jesus has indeed shared with us his own privilege of being able to call God in the way only he could call him: *Abba, Father*! 'Father' is God's name because this is what he does, this is what delights him – to keep on *fathering us*.

However, it would be wrong to think that when Jesus teaches us to call God 'father' he invites us to see him by referring to our own earthly father. God is Father in a unique way, unlike any other father on earth. God is Father in the way Jesus revealed to us: he sheds the light of the sun and pours the blessing of rain on the just and the unjust;[4] even as he feeds the birds of the air and clothes the lilies in the fields,

[4] Mt. 5.45.

so much more does he take loving care of each one of us;[5] he knows everything we need;[6] he gives good things to those who ask for them;[7] just as no sparrow falls to the ground unperceived by him, so are we of such value to him that he has counted even the number of the hairs on our head;[8] it is his will that nobody, not even the least of us, should be lost;[9] he wants to grant to us everything we ask and especially his own Spirit, his love;[10] he is forgiving;[11] we have nothing to fear because he finds pleasure in rescuing us;[12] he is filled with compassion for us, puts his arms around us, kisses us, does not even want to let us say how sorry we are to have scorned his love: he is filled with joy when we are restored to him again;[13] he does not judge anyone;[14] no evil can snatch us from the safety and protection of his hand.[15]

This is God's name, this is the way in which his name is hallowed or glorified: his name is Father and

[5] Mt. 6.26.
[6] Mt. 6.32.
[7] Mt. 7.11.
[8] Mt. 10.29f.
[9] Mt. 18.14.
[10] Mt. 18.19; Lk. 11.13.
[11] Lk. 6.36.
[12] Lk. 12.32.
[13] Cf. Lk. 15.11–24.
[14] Jn 5.22.
[15] Jn 10.29.

he finds glory, joy and pleasure in fathering us in these ways. Thus, when I say: *hallowed be thy name* I mean: 'Father, keep fathering me.'

Indeed, 'Father' is the name that protects us: *Holy Father, protect in your name those you have given me, so that they may be one, as we are one.*[16] The Father glorifies himself by making us one with the Son he loves, and he protects us, so that we *may all be one as you, Father, are in me and I am in you*.

Therefore, a new day has arrived. This day began the moment Jesus taught us the *Our Father*, the moment he taught us what kind of Father God is and wants to be to us, and how confidently we can ask him anything.

> 'On that day you will not need to ask anything of me' – says Jesus – 'because very truly, I tell you, if you ask anything directly to the Father in my name, he will give it to you . . . Ask and you will receive, so that your joy may be complete . . . for the Father himself loves you, because you have loved me and have believed that I came from God.'[17]

[16] Jn 17.11.
[17] Cf. Jn 16.26–27.

A NEW HEART

God's name is *Father*. This name is *hallowed* when we allow God to be our Father, to pour his fatherly love on us, to *father* us. When we call the Father's name he can again act in our favour. Not that he had stopped acting in our favour when we were ignoring him: he continued to give us *life, movement and being*,[1] and went on *commanding his angels to guard us in all our ways*,[2] he kept waiting for us. But like the prodigal son, we were *in a distant country*,[3] and the Father could not give us our daily bread, forgive us our sins and stand by us in the time of trial.

This should help us to understand the third sentence of the *Our Father, Your kingdom come*. Just as a king truly is such, *king*, if he can reign, if he can make use of his wisdom and justice to guarantee the peace and the prosperity of his people, so our Father truly is *ours* and truly is *Father* when he can *father us*, when

[1] Acts 17.28.
[2] Ps. 91.11.
[3] Lk. 15.13.

he can act in our favour. Thus the first two sentences of the *Our Father* – *hallowed be thy name* and *thy kingdom come* – in fact say the same thing.

The image of the *kingdom* in Scripture has a further nuance: it points not only to God acting in our favour, but to the fact that he does this in a *decisive way*, in a final way, in a way that settles it. Throughout the history of the people of Israel, God had taken action in their favour by freeing them from the slavery of the Egyptians, by giving them bread from heaven and water from a rock, by introducing them into a promised land, by protecting them from their enemies. But all these actions were never decisive, final: once he had freed the people of Israel from one enemy, God had to protect them from some other threat.

More deeply so, however, God wanted to free his people not only from the enemies without, but especially from the enemy within: idolatry, the slavery to a false image of God that prevented them from trusting their Father entirely and explained why they kept trying to find refuge either in their own strength or in alliances with other nations that in the end would always turn against them.

This is why God's decisive action in favour of his people is not only peace without, but peace within;

not first of all political freedom, but freedom of the heart: 'A new heart I will give you, and a new spirit I will put within you; I will remove from your body the heart of stone and give you a heart of flesh.'[4] This is the core meaning of the two first sentences of the *Our Father*: *hallowed be thy name* and *thy kingdom come*. They both mean: 'Father, take this decisive action in our favour you have promised through Ezekiel: give us a new heart!'

We need a new heart. And it is patient and persevering prayer on our part that allows the Father to give it to us. Of course, this transformation is not effected through magic, nor is it something of which we are merely passive recipients.

The Father works this wonder by establishing a new covenant with us, by inviting us into a new way of being in relation with him based on a deeper knowledge of his real identity. *Nobody had ever seen God*, certainly nobody had ever imagined how far he was prepared to go on our behalf, until Jesus came and *made the Father known to us.*[5]

The way Jesus changed our hearts, the way he showed the Father's love for us, was by living with

[4] Ezek. 36.28.
[5] Cf. Jn 1.18.

us. The first thing he did when he started his ministry was to surround himself with disciples, to call
them friends and bear patiently with their stubborn-
ness, their inability to understand him, their desires
for human glory, their squabbles, their treasons, their
denials. He did this *to show them the full extent of his
love*,[6] of the Father's love *for them*. This is why they
were the only ones who could be his witnesses after
his resurrection, the only ones who could really tell
the world who God, who the Father really is: they had
*been with Jesus the whole time he went in and out among
them*;[7] their eyes had seen, their hands had touched,
their ears had heard and their hearts had felt this joy
of being loved until the end,[8] they had experienced
this decisive, this decisively persuading action of God
in their favour, their heart had indeed been changed,
they had finally allowed the Father to love them and
had become somehow able to love him in return.

The same thing happens through patient and persevering prayer, too; this is the bread we ask for in
prayer: the Father's love and consolation. And this is
why this bread has to be asked for every day: *Give us*

[6] Cf. Jn 13.1.
[7] Acts 1.21.
[8] Cf. 1 Jn 1.1–4 and Jn 13.1.

today our daily bread. Love is not a bread to eat once in passing. We need to receive and savour it daily. We need to welcome it every day: *O that today you would listen to his voice and not harden your hearts!*[9]

Prayer is listening to the voice of the Spirit within us who daily fills our hearts with love, joy, peace, patience and kindness.[10] Through prayer we dwell with Jesus and allow him to dwell in us: *Remain in me and I will remain in you . . . Remain in my love. I tell you this so that my joy may be in you and your joy may be complete.*[11] Prayer is the therapy through which our hearts of stone are progressively turned into hearts of flesh because prayer is simply remaining in the presence of the Lord just as flowers remain exposed to the light of the sun that sustains their life.

Our request for this bread needs renewing *daily*, for however much we may be loved by the Lord, however many times we may have experienced his faithfulness and his mercy, our need remains. Just like flowers, the moment we stop turning to the sun we start withering. It took Peter a long, long time and many setbacks to finally learn this lesson. He kept presuming on his

[9] Ps. 95.7–8.
[10] Gal. 5.22.
[11] Cf. Jn 15.4, 9, 11.

love for the Lord, kept promising a faithfulness and a commitment he was totally incapable of: *Peter said: I will lay down my life for you. Jesus answered: You will lay down your life for me? I tell you . . . you will disown me over and over again!*[12]

This is not just Peter, this is us. We cannot help disowning the Lord in one way or the other, whether out of negligence or weakness, whether by trying to own him to our advantage or by ignoring him. The good news is not that our heart will be changed once for all, but that it can be changed every day. Every day our patient Father will give us the daily bread of forgiveness and love, of tenderness and comfort, of the patience and strength we need in our journey with him. And no matter how many times we might be tempted to presume of our love for him, he will keep probing us until we reach that posture of humility that keeps us open to him, just as he did with Peter.

He kept asking him, *'Simon son of Jonas, do you love me?'* . . . *'Simon son of Jonas, do you love me?'* – and each time Peter would reply: *Yes Lord, you know that!* But this answer was not enough for Jesus and so he kept asking: *'Simon son of Jonas, do you love me?'* until Peter

[12] Cf. Jn 13.37–38.

gets it and erupts in this most splendid of answers:
'*Lord, you know everything; you know that I love you.*'[13]

'You know Lord that indeed I will keep presuming
on myself, on my love for you; I will keep alternating
between bursts of enthusiasm and times of discouragement and guilt; I will keep disowning you in one
way or another . . . But I now know that my hope for
faithfulness lies not in me but in you and I will keep
begging daily for forgiveness and for love, asking
to the Father as you taught us: may your kingdom
come, take action in my favour, give me the daily
bread of love and forgiveness and tenderness and
hope that keeps my heart new!'

[13] Jn 21.15ff.

AS FOR ME, I TRUST IN YOU

The key to the *Our Father* is not to be found in its words, but in the posture it teaches us to embrace in God's presence, in our dealings with God. We find an unexpected confirmation of this in the fact that the text of the *Our Father* is given only in the Gospels of Matthew and Luke. In the versions of the good news by Mark and by John this essential hallmark of Christian life is absent. How is this possible? How can they have overlooked this aspect of Jesus' teaching? How can anyone who wants to give a fair account of the novelty Jesus has introduced on earth neglect to mention the prayer which lies at the heart of our Christian identity?

Let us focus our inquiry on Mark's Gospel. The shortest among the Gospels, Mark has often been seen as the most rudimentary, something like a first draft on which Matthew and Luke are supposed to have improved. Even though it comes after Matthew in our Gospels, researchers unanimously agree on considering Mark as the oldest Gospel, dating it back to the decade that immediately followed Jesus' death, around the year AD 45. Mark chose concision, not ironing out the discrepancies of his sources, and is fond of aphorisms that can be read at a very prosaic level and yet are pregnant with deeper meanings.

One example of this is Jesus saying to his disciples, *Let us go on to the neighbouring towns, so that I may proclaim the message there also; for that is what I came out to do.*[1] The obvious meaning of this sentence is that Jesus came out of the village to go elsewhere, but we are also entitled to understand that proclaiming the good news was the reason why Jesus came out from the bosom of the Father and planted his tent among us, in a way parallel to what John says in the Prologue of his Gospel: *The Word [the Son of God] became flesh and lived among us; he came to . . . give to all who welcomed him and believed in him the power to become children of God.*[2]

In another instance, to raise a young girl from the dead Jesus goes all the way to her room, takes her by the hand and says to her, *Talitha Koum, little girl, I say to you, get up.*[3] This evocative action gives us a glimpse of the Risen Jesus descending into hell, *to*

[1] Mk 1.38.
[2] Cf. Jn 1.14, 16.
[3] Mk 5.41.

make a proclamation to the spirits in prison, in Peter's words:[4] having defeated death once for all, he takes Adam and Eve by the hand and brings them back to life everlasting.

Most commentators today agree on considering Mark's Gospel a literary gem, and one detail in particular militates in favour of this view. It is Mark who conceived the literary genre of 'Gospels', which is unlike anything that had been written before. He was the first to face the daunting task of having to describe the most extraordinary event that ever happened in human history and to relay a message of everlasting significance. As another Gospel writer who had to take up the same challenge half a century afterwards says: *there are so many things that Jesus did that if every one of them were written down, the world itself could not contain the books that would be written.*[5] Mark's genius was to see that concision would suit something so vast and deep better than prolixity; its meaning would be conveyed best by suggesting it rather than by trying to describe it in an exhaustive way.

So he summed up everything in some twenty pages in which words and actions are conveyed in

[4] Pet. 3.19.
[5] Jn 21.25.

pithy sentences, elliptical aphorisms and crisp little descriptions. One is reminded of Michelangelo's famous later sculptures, the *Awakening Slave*, the *Young Slave*, the *Bearded Slave*, the *Atlas* and especially his unrivalled *Pietà Rondanini*, which barely sketch the figures he believed were already contained in the marble. As in the case of Mark's Gospel, the immense evocative power of these shapes comes precisely from the fact that they suggest more than they describe and appeal to the viewer's or the reader's imagination and understanding.

This also applies to Mark's version of Jesus' teaching about prayer. Mark could not have ignored the *Our Father*. He is believed to have relied on the witness of the Apostle Peter as his main source and he must have been told of the crucial significance of this prayer. However, instead of simply recounting the event and the words of the *Our Father*, he chose to focus on the posture this prayer was intended to enshrine. Had he simply quoted the text of the *Our Father*, his readers might have considered it merely as a prayer, as one prayer among others, maybe the highest of prayers, but still only one among many. To prevent this possible misunderstanding, he decided to focus on the posture we have described earlier with the help of one of his favourite literary devices useful for dealing with truths too deep for words alone: he told a little story, a sort of allegory.

Thus are we prepared to tackle the perplexing episode located towards the end of his Gospel, during Jesus' last days before his death, when he preaches in Jerusalem during the day, but he is forced to spend the night outside its walls in Bethany because the scribes and Pharisees are trying to arrest him and have him killed. One morning, as Jesus and his disciples were on their way back to Jerusalem from Bethany, he was hungry, saw in the distance a fig tree in leaf and went to see whether perhaps he would find anything on it. When he came to it, he found nothing but leaves, for it was not the season for figs. He said to it, 'May no one ever eat fruit from you again.' And his disciples heard it.[6]

This incident is the prelude to the climax in the ongoing confrontation between Jesus and the Jewish religious authorities. That same day, in Jerusalem, Jesus drove out of the temple those who were buying and selling there, overturned the tables of the money-changers and the benches of the dove-sellers. Significantly, the saying that accompanies this action

[6] Mk 11.12ff.

concerns prayer: *My house will be called a house of prayer for all nations, but you have made it a den of robbers.*[7]

The inability or unwillingness of the fig tree to yield its fruits had been a recurrent analogy in the Old Testament: 'When I wanted to gather my people, says the Lord, there are no grapes on the vine, nor figs on the fig tree; even the leaves are withered, and what I gave them has passed away from them.'[8]

The withering which Mark attributes to Jesus' curse in reality results from the people's decision to go their own way, from their refusal to listen to the Lord, from their idolatry. Just as when the roots are cut off from the water the tree dies, so when the people severs its relation with the Lord, dispersion ensues: *Ephraim is stricken, their root is dried up, they bear no fruit . . . Because they have not listened to my God . . . they shall become wanderers among the nations.*[9]

[7] Mk 11.17.
[8] Jer. 8.13. Cf. Hab. 3.17–19: 'Though the fig tree does not blossom, and no fruit is on the vines; though the produce of the olive fails and the fields yield no food; though the flock is cut off from the fold and there is no herd in the stalls, yet I will rejoice in the Lord; I will exult in the God of my salvation. God, the Lord, is my strength; he makes my feet like the feet of a deer, and makes me tread upon the heights'.
[9] Hos. 9.16–17.

Mark links the withering of the fig tree to the fact that prayer had been replaced by robbery; a loving, thankful and free relation with the Lord, giver of life, had been stifled by an exploitation of religion for financial and political interests. Instead of hallowing the Father's name they used it to their own advantage.

No surprise therefore if the following day as Jesus and his disciples again pass by the fig tree on their way to Jerusalem they find it *withered away to its roots*. When Peter notices this, Jesus answers with the teaching on prayer that is Mark's version of the *Our Father*:

> 'Have faith in God. Truly I tell you, if you say to this mountain, "Be taken up and thrown into the sea", and if you do not doubt in your heart, but believe that what you say will come to pass, it will be done for you. So I tell you, whatever you ask for in prayer, believe that you have received it, and it will be yours. Whenever you stand praying, forgive, if you have anything against anyone; so that your Father in heaven may also forgive you your trespasses.'[10]

Of course, the power of prayer praised in this passage is not meant to explain the effectiveness of Jesus' curse

[10] Mk 11.22–25.

on the fig tree. This would not make any sense. God loves his creation, he takes care of the lilies of the field and feeds the birds of the air[11] and would never hurt any of the living things he himself creates and sustains. It is rather the contrary. However fatal and irredeemable the withering of a tree can seem, however incurable the hardening of our heart in our relation to God may have become, however tempted we might be to think that evil has won, Jesus keeps reminding us that *for mortals it is impossible, but for God all things are possible.*[12] Here, moreover, Jesus points to prayer as one of the potential instruments of God's action: because everything is possible to God, then everything is possible to prayer, or rather, to a certain kind of prayer, a prayer that expresses a particular *posture* in God's presence.

This is why Mark's passage focuses only on the posture that makes everything possible to prayer: the example of a mountain thrown into the sea is an image of just how effective prayer can be provided that it is pitched right. The right pitch, the right posture, is described here in this cry: *Have faith in God!*

[11] Mt. 6.25–26.
[12] Mt. 19.26.

It takes the heart of a child who knows that God is his loving Father to muster up such faith, such trust in him. It takes a heart in tune with the prayer of the Holy Spirit that probes the depths of God to believe in this way. In whichever way we might pray, whatever words we may use, whatever method we follow, that which gives wings to prayer, that which enables it to obtain anything from the Father, is this unshakeable trust: *So I tell you, whatever you ask for in prayer, believe that you have received it, and it will be yours.*[13]

Mark did not need to quote the exact words of the *Our Father* because the secret to the Christian approach to prayer is not to be looked for in formulas, in methods, in techniques, nor in the ability to focus, in the place we choose, or in the length of time we devote to it. Once again, all these factors may have their importance, but they can just as well mislead us if they distract us from what prayer is, what lies at the heart of it. Prayer is all about trust in God, a trust full of hope and desire, a loving trust. Prayer is all about entrusting ourselves, our lives and our cause to the Father.

The depth of our prayer depends on the depth of our trust in God; our ability to persevere in prayer

[13] Mk 11.24.

depends on the endurance of our trust; our determination to cling to God depends on the strength of
our trust. Of course, the reverse is also true: trust
feeds prayer, but prayer in return feeds trust – just
as the more time I spend with the person I love the
deeper grows my connection to him or her.

The Psalms, those inspired poems that have nour-
ished the prayer of innumerable generations of
believers, are all about affirming this trust, nurturing
it, finding our joy and our peace in it. Each one of
the following sentences can feed our prayer for hours,
simply repeated:

> Those who know your name trust in you, for you,
> Lord, have never forsaken those who seek you.[14]
>
> But I trust in your unfailing love; my heart rejoices
> in your salvation.[15]
>
> Some trust in chariots and some in horses, but we
> trust in the name of the Lord our God.[16]
>
> In you, Lord my God, I put my trust. I trust in
> you, do not let me be put to shame, nor let my
> enemies triumph over me.[17]
>
> But I trust in you, Lord, I say, 'You are my God.'[18]

[14] Ps. 9.10.
[15] Ps. 13.5.
[16] Ps. 20.7.
[17] Ps. 25.1–2.
[18] Ps. 31.14.

But I am like an olive tree flourishing in the house of God; I trust in God's unfailing love for ever and ever.[19]

But as for me, I trust in you.[20]

When I am afraid, I put my trust in you. In God, whose word I praise – in God I trust and am not afraid.[21]

Trust in him at all times, you people; pour out your hearts to him, for God is our refuge.[22]

Bring joy to your servant, Lord, for I put my trust in you.[23]

I will say of the Lord, 'He is my refuge and my fortress, my God, in whom I trust.'[24]

Let the morning bring me word of your unfailing love, for I have put my trust in you. Show me the way I should go, for to you I entrust my life.[25]

[19] Ps. 52.8.
[20] Ps. 55.23.
[21] Ps. 56.3–4.
[22] Ps. 62.8.
[23] Ps. 86.4.
[24] Ps. 91.2.
[25] Ps. 143.8.

THROWING MOUNTAINS
IN THE SEA

To those who might be tempted to see prayer as a form of passivity, of neglecting one's responsibility to act, of finding pretexts for delaying action, Jesus' teaching could not present a starker refutation than this cinematic image of throwing mountains into the sea! We must acknowledge that few spiritual treatises have ever come up with the idea of defining prayer in this way. And yet this is how we are invited to see the impact of prayer, to believe in its ability to alter the landscape so dramatically that even when our horizon is irredeemably barred, even when our path is blocked by something as bulky as a mountain, we must never give way to hopelessness or despair, but keep on praying, keep on *hoping against hope*.[1]

Now, according to Jesus, the most formidable of all mountains, the greatest challenge we are bound to face in our Christian life, the bulkiest hindrance

[1] Rom. 4.18.

on our way, the darkest cloud on our horizon, is our inability to forgive.

This emerges from a close reading of what we have called Mark's version of the *Our Father*, that is the passage of his Gospel where we are given the posture implied by Jesus' prayer even if we do not find the words he taught to his disciples in it.

This text consists of three parallel sentences.[2]

The first two sentences concern prayers which are fulfilled because of the faith that underpins them. The first sentence says: 'if you say to this mountain, "Be taken up and thrown into the sea", and if you do not doubt in your heart, but believe that what you say will come to pass, it will be done for you'.

The second tells us that 'whatever you ask for in prayer, believe that you have received it, and it will be yours'.

The third echoes the first sentence in that it deals with another mountain that prevents prayer from lifting up our heart and soul, i.e. the fact of having something against someone, of having been the

[2] Mk 11.22–25: 'Have faith in God. Truly I tell you, (1) if you say to this mountain, "Be taken up and thrown into the sea", and if you do not doubt in your heart, but believe that what you say will come to pass, it will be done for you. So I tell you, (2) whatever you ask for in prayer, believe that you have received it, and it will be yours. (3) Whenever you stand praying, forgive, if you have anything against anyone; so that your Father in heaven may also forgive you your trespasses.'

object of some wrong or injustice from somebody and of being hurt and unable to forgive because of this. This is the mountain which prayer throws into the sea when the wrong or injustice we have received is forgiven.

In the last sentence the parallel with the *Our Father* comes openly to the fore since we have a quotation of one of the petitions of Matthew's version of Jesus' prayer: *forgive us our debts as we also forgive our debtors*.[3] Even more significantly, however, Mark's sentence echoes Jesus' own commentary of the *Our Father* according to Matthew's version. What is the key aspect of the *Our Father* for Jesus? Jesus' answer leaves no doubt: *For if you forgive others their trespasses, your heavenly Father will also forgive you; but if you do not forgive others, neither will your Father forgive your trespasses*.[4] Prayer for Jesus is about throwing into the sea the mountain that prevents us from having access to true forgiveness.

We should therefore ask ourselves: why is forgiveness so important? Why is it so crucial for prayer? Why does Jesus focus on it so dramatically?

[3] Mt. 6.12; cf. Lk. 11.4.
[4] Mt. 6.14–15.

The answer is very simple: because it is a mountain in its own way, it is every bit as heavy, as immovable, as insurmountable, as a physical mountain. Here we have to leave behind our idyllic image of mountains as places where we can go for a walk and enjoy a wonderful view. Instead, we should picture a rockface impossible to climb and with no way round it: our journey to wherever we were heading is over before it started.

Forgiveness is a rock-face, a mountain which it is not in our power to climb and with no way round it. Trying simply to excuse those who hurt us, or confining ourselves to ignoring our enemies or stopping short of hatred, is not forgiveness. When we have been really hurt by somebody, when the wrong we have suffered has left deep scars in our flesh and painful consequences in our life, true forgiveness simply is impossible, it goes against our fundamental instincts of survival, it would amount to a sort of death.

In no other areas of Christian life do we experience our powerlessness more humiliatingly than with forgiveness. It is impossible to hear what the Gospel says about it without being filled by a sense of discouragement. No matter how many times we try to forgive, try not to react to evil, try not to give in to resentment, it is always just as hard. We might be able to overcome animosity or negative thoughts for a while, but at some point our heart hardens and bitterness again takes over; or we succeed outwardly, but in our heart we cannot help still disliking the person who hurt us, avoiding or even slandering him or her. We continue to be cold, distant, indifferent, or, worse, we find ourselves rejoicing when those who have done us a bad turn suffer and something ugly happens to them: we are tempted to see this as a just punishment. Acknowledging this sad experience is crucial – we have to accept that forgiving, forgiving truly and evangelically, is far from easy.

There are two possible reactions to the challenge of Jesus' teaching about forgiveness. One reaction would be to consider it as hyperbole, a rhetorical exaggeration: Jesus is not really asking us to turn the other cheek, or to leave our cloak. These should be interpreted as overstatements typical of Semitic language, as when Jesus says: *If your right eye causes you to sin, pluck it out and cast it from you.*[5] The other reaction would be to take Jesus' teaching about forgiveness as a mere moral injunction: he says that I must forgive

[5] Mt. 5.29; 18.9.

my enemies and love them, so I just have to do it –
take the decision and put it into practice. If I have not
succeeded so far, if I have been unable to forgive, it is
because I did not really try. Both these reactions, both
these ways of understanding the Gospel message, are
wrong.

First, we have Jesus' example to tell us that this
is not hyperbole. True, he never plucked out his eye,
nor did he ask anyone else to do such a thing – that
is a genuine case of rhetorical exaggeration. But he
set us a clear example with forgiveness. He offered
no resistance to those who arrested, tortured and
killed him; he continued to love Judas and washed
his feet at the last supper, he gave his life for him, he
offered his cheek to his kiss of betrayal, as he did to
the soldiers who slapped him; to those who dragged
him into court he gave no answer, he did not defend
himself, knowing that they were not seeking the truth
and that it was useless to talk; on the cross he prayed
for his killers and obtained for them forgiveness from
the Father: *Father forgive them for they know not what
they do.*[6] So Jesus' teaching about forgiveness contains
no rhetorical exaggeration. The example of Jesus
shows us that it must be taken literally.

[6] Lk. 23.34.

But a moralistic stance that made forgiveness purely a matter of will would be just as wrong because it is impossible to forgive. At best, we might be capable of 'getting over it', but this is not forgiveness, because hostility, grudge, resentment remain buried in us and at the right time they will come to the surface again, perhaps even amplified. Jesus' teaching about forgiveness goes much deeper than this. In fact, the gospel teaches us that our hearts become able to forgive only when we raise our eyes and meet the eyes of our Father who is in heaven.

We do not have access to forgiveness through an act of will, but through a patient and often lengthy process in which prayer plays the key role, as Jesus clearly indicates when he says to us: *Pray for your enemies.*[7] Indeed, in Matthew's Gospel, the process of forgiving starts by turning our gaze to the Father *who makes his sun rise on the evil and on the good, and sends rain on the just and on the unjust.*[8] Only the Lord, only the Father, *forgives us all our iniquities and heals us from all our diseases*[9] — and what greater disease do we need to be healed from than the grip of pride, resentment and

[7] Mt. 5.44.
[8] Mt. 5.45.
[9] Ps. 103.2–3.

animosity? Whoever has received from God the grace of forgiving has experienced this: it is like a knot that is suddenly undone, like a huge weight removed from our heart, like a mountain thrown into the sea. It is no accident that freedom from bitterness and resentment often manifests itself through a flow of tears, not tears of sorrow or sadness but of liberation and joy.

It is crucial therefore fully to appreciate what a threatening and insurmountable mountain forgiveness is and, at the same time, the extent to which it is impossible from a human viewpoint. This acknowledgment is essential because blaming ourselves for our unforgiving attitude and feeling guilty about it would only make the situation worse.

Whenever we experience our inability to forgive, whenever we experience how painful it is not only to grant forgiveness, but then to maintain it, especially when we are exposed to the enduring consequences of the injury we have received, we should not feel discouraged but welcome this humiliation. Often the person who hurt us, the 'enemy', remains an enemy, a threat. Balancing authentic forgiveness with fair self-defence is a tricky business; keeping the heart clean from resentment and the eye clear from distorted perceptions of reality is a constant exercise that has to be renewed daily. This resistance of our heart to forgiveness is a humiliation that paradoxically benefits our spiritual life because through it we experience in our flesh our dependence on God, our need for God, the fact that without God we cannot do anything.

There are many fields of Christian life, many aspects of Christian behaviour, where we can more or less easily persuade ourselves that we are not that bad after all, that with a bit of effort, of imagination and good will we can manage: talking or writing persuasively in spiritual matters, preaching with success, even serving the poor. Our motives for doing good might be mixed, but the job is done and some good comes out of it. One thing we cannot simulate in this way is forgiveness. Forgiveness is and remains a pure grace, an undeserved gift, the most unmistakeable trait of authentic conversion, the one thing we can never fake, because our heart will know the truth.

We have repeatedly said that the fundamental law of prayer is that *We do not know how to pray*, and as this is a continuing state we need to remain tuned into the prayer of the Holy Spirit, itself for ever continuing in our hearts. Exactly the same is true of the fundamental law of forgiveness: 'We are unable to forgive', because forgiving is not just a choice made at one precise moment of our life, it has to be ongoing – forgiving is 'to keep forgiving', day after day. Forgiving, too, is a bread we have to beg daily from the Lord: 'Give us today our daily ability to forgive.'

Our inability to forgive is the structural humiliation we need as Christians to keep us praying, to keep begging. If I do not feel this need, this inability, this humiliation, I do not pray. My prayer can remain lukewarm and uncommitted for years until at one moment I am faced with the need to forgive for something wrong, something hurtful, something that lacerates my insides. Then I find myself at a crossroads: if I want to be a Christian I have to forgive and for this I have to pray, to knock, to beg, to ask – then I start praying for real, at last.

DELAYS

One of the distinctive features of a Christian in the
New Testament is an attitude, a way of positioning
oneself in relation to the Father and to everything
else, which is conveyed by the Greek word *parrhesia*,
literally outspokenness and hence frankness, blunt-
ness, assurance. This word is used for example in the
book of Acts to describe the new boldness Jesus' disciples acquired after they received the gift of the Holy
Spirit.[1] The same people who had lived hidden in the
upper room for over a month after Jesus had been
killed because they were afraid of the Jewish leaders[2] suddenly emerged speaking in Jesus' name and
started preaching to the crowds, no longer afraid to
defy the ban against this,[3] full of assurance when they
were dragged before judges and tribunals.[4] This came
as a great surprise to everyone: 'When they saw the
boldness of Peter and John and realized that they were

[1] Cf. Acts 2.29; 4.13, 29, 31; 28.31.
[2] Jn 20.19.
[3] Acts 5.40ff.
[4] Acts 5.27–32.

uneducated and ordinary men, they were amazed and recognized them as companions of Jesus.'[5]

But *parrhesia* also describes the way in which Christians can approach the Father, talk with him and pray to him. It is difficult for us to imagine how unthinkable it was for people brought up in a pagan culture to be told that they did not need any mediation between them and God but that they could talk to him directly, confidently, freely, like a child with its father. Dealings with the divinities in a pagan environment are thoroughly codified. Nobody can take the risk of acting spontaneously in this field because he might offend the divinity even unwillingly and this would have unforeseeable consequences. Whatever might have qualified as prayer in a pagan environment was dominated by guilt, anxiety and fear.

Christianity reached pagan culture and religiosity as gospel, as 'good news', precisely because of the freedom it brought to people: freedom from the mediation of priestly figures who used religion to their advantage as an instrument of power; freedom from the multiplicity of codes and rules that were laid on people's shoulders on the pretext that these

[5] Acts 4.13.

ensured their safety in their dealings with divinities. Above all it brought freedom from guilt, anxiety and fear in their relationship with God: *Indeed the Lord is the Spirit, and where the Spirit of the Lord is, there is freedom . . . Since, then, we have such a hope, we can act with great boldness.*[6] The Father's love has dispelled fear: *There is no fear in love, but perfect love casts out fear.*[7] We now trust God as a Father and we have free access to him *in boldness and confidence.*[8]

It is especially the letter to the Hebrews, one of the most elaborate and fascinating writings of the New Testament, which insists on this point. It is a highly allegorical book where God is represented as a king on a throne, not to stress his greatness or distance from us, but on the contrary to emphasize the privilege we have been granted in the form of free access to him: we can *approach the throne of grace with boldness, to receive mercy and find help in time of need.*[9] We now have such *confidence* that we can *approach* the Father *with a true heart in full assurance . . . without wavering, for he who has promised is faithful.*[10]

[6] Cor. 3.12, 17.
[7] Jn 4.18.
[8] Eph. 3.12.
[9] Heb. 4.16.
[10] Heb. 10.19–23.

Whatever happens in our lives, we must hold fast to this boldness, to this confidence: *Do not, therefore, abandon that confidence of yours; it brings a great reward.*[11] Even when our hearts surrender to guilt, when we are harsh on ourselves or condemn ourselves, we are invited to *reassure our hearts before him because God is greater than our hearts, and he knows everything.* Then our *hearts will not condemn us* any more because we have this *boldness before God.*[12]

All this has a direct impact on prayer, on the way we can address God: our assurance is such that we trust we shall *receive from him whatever we ask,*[13] because we know that *he hears us. And if we know that he hears us in whatever we ask, we know that we have obtained the requests made of him.*[14]

The authenticity of our conversion, the depth of our spiritual life as Christians, can be measured by the boldness and the assurance of our prayer. Our Christian life is only as authentic as our prayer is bold and confident, well beyond what we are inclined to imagine or dare. We can say that our boldness and confidence will never match the extent to which God

[11] Heb 10.35.
[12] Jn 3.18–22.
[13] Jn 3.18–22.
[14] Jn 5.14–17.

wants to give us all we could ever want. We read these words and we think 'OK, I've got it' when in reality 'No you haven't got it: You think you have, but you haven't . . .'

The real tragedy of Christian life is how little trust we are ready to place in God, and indeed in prayer – how little in fact we are prepared to ask of him. Even more depressingly, it is sad to see how little imagination we give God credit for.

Who would think it worth bringing God into those aspects of our life which we consider too small, too secular, too practical or simply too personal?

A girl agonizing over a seemingly doomed relationship with a boy longs for some relief, she prays about it, and gets a smile or a sign of friendship from this boy. Who would give importance to the melodrama of an adolescent love story? Who would think it worth bringing God into it? Well, God does, the Father does, Jesus who says *everything you ask in prayer* . . .[15] – everything! We will never tire of repeating something already stated earlier: God is sincerely, deeply interested in each one of our thoughts, our worries, our feelings and our hurts – none, absolutely none, is too small for him. He assures us of

[15] Mk 11.22–25.

this. Do we know the number of hairs on our head? No? Well, the Father does! None of it is too small for him.[16] And he collects each and every one of our tears to wipe them away[17] and console us.

This point needs further probing. A Christian is someone who has to be bold and confident in prayer. This was Jesus' own teaching in what we have called Mark's version of the *Our Father*, where he declares: *So I tell you, whatever you ask for in prayer, believe that you have received it, and it will be yours.*[18] It all amounts to how outspoken, how frank, how candid, how daring we are when we pray. Jesus says *whatever you ask for in prayer will be yours*. But how far does this promise go? Is it really true that we can obtain from God *whatever* we ask of him?

If we confine our search to Mark's Gospel, we come across a number of instances where boldness, assurance and insolence in prayer are indeed not only rewarded but even praised.

Lepers according to the Old Testament rules had to live outside the city, alone. They could not even come near any healthy person and for this reason had

[16] Mt. 10.30 and Lk. 12.7.
[17] Rev. 21.4.
[18] Mk 11.24.

to cry 'Unclean, unclean' all the time.[19] But here we see a leper approaching Jesus, kneeling before him, begging him insistently: *If you choose, you can make me clean*. This is one of the rare instances in which the Gospel affirms that Jesus was affected, that some sort of deep and stirring emotion shook him, which curiously the different manuscripts describe using two opposite Greek verbs: according to one tradition Jesus is said to have been filled with compassion and to another tradition he was filled with anger. In any case, this means that the leper's request touched something in Jesus, that it possessed something which Jesus could not resist, so that he stretched out his hand and touched him, and said to him, 'I do choose. Be made clean!' and immediately the leprosy left him, and he was made clean.[20]

We meet an even more striking instance of the power of a trusting and bold prayer over Jesus with the case of a *woman who had been suffering from haemorrhages for twelve years*.[21] She was desperate: *she had endured much under many physicians, and despite having spent all that she had she was no better, but rather grew worse*. Her

19 Lev. 13.45–46.
20 Mk 1.40–45.
21 Mk 5.25–34.

faith and her trust were such, she was so certain that God could not but listen to her prayer, that she was not deterred by the crowd surrounding Jesus and by the consequent impossibility of getting his attention: she *came up behind him in the crowd and touched his cloak, for she said, 'If I but touch his clothes, I will be made well.'*

This leads to one of the most startling episodes reported in the New Testament. The Gospel emphasizes that the result is immediate: *Immediately her haemorrhage stopped; and she felt in her body that she was healed of her disease.* The extraordinary thing, however, is that Jesus himself is surprised by what has happened: 'Immediately aware that a power had gone forth from him, Jesus turned round in the crowd and said, "Who touched my clothes?" And his disciples said to him, "You see the crowd pressing in on you; how can you say, 'Who touched me?'"' The woman's trust had been such that somehow she had been granted access to Jesus' own power even before he agreed to this. No magic, of course, is involved here. We know that the woman would not have been able to do this, that she would not have had that trust, that she would not have come near Jesus, unless the Father had drawn her.[22]

[22] Jn 6.44.

It is rather puzzling however to see Jesus asking who had done this and *looking all round to see who had done it* since we know he was able to read people's thoughts.[23]

The scene is striking. A large crowd shouting, pressing in on Jesus, noise and confusion – and suddenly all this movement freezes and fades into the background, the camera zooms in on Jesus and the woman, a special kind of connection has united them instantaneously: *the woman, knowing what had happened to her, came in fear and trembling, fell down before him, and told him the whole truth.* She had touched Jesus. Of course, many people were touching Jesus at that moment, but the way the woman touched him was different.

There is only one thing that really touches him, that touches the Father, and this is bold, confident prayer – a prayer that dares everything, that does not stop at anything. This trust somehow has power over God. We see an admiring Jesus drawing near the kneeling woman, taking her face in both his hands, looking into her eyes and whispering to her: *Daughter, your faith has made you well; go in peace, and be healed of your disease.* This miracle is the result of faith, of a prayer that has summoned up the woman's whole heart, soul and

[23] Mk 2.8.

strength. It is the result of a prayer led by the Holy Spirit who searches the depths of God and knows what God wants. Prayer can indeed *touch* God.

But prayer can go further, it has to. We must never lose heart. However hopeless our cause might seem, we must keep asking, knocking, praying. *Jesus told them a parable about their need to keep praying and not to lose heart*;[24] this is the colourful parable of the judge who *neither feared God nor had respect for people* but in the end was forced to cave in to a widow's tenacity:

> There was a widow who kept coming to him and saying, 'Grant me justice against my opponent.' For a while he refused; but later he said to himself, 'Though I have no fear of God and no respect for anyone, yet because this widow keeps bothering me, I will grant her justice, so that she may not wear me out by continually coming.'

As a commentary on this story, Jesus adds: *Listen to what the unjust judge says. And will not God grant justice to his chosen ones who cry to him day and night? Will he delay long in helping them?*[25] The idea of God delaying his decision to come to our help can be disturbing.

[24] Lk. 18.1–8.
[25] Lk. 18.6–7.

If he can come to our help, why does he not do so immediately? Is he a detached observer? Is he unmoved by our struggle? Has his help somehow to be deserved by persistent request or by a sufficiently eager desire?

It is always good to remember that the Father so loved us that he sent his only Son.[26] The Lord knows our suffering: *But you do see! Indeed you note trouble and grief, that you may take it into your hands; the helpless commit themselves to you; you have been the helper of the orphan.*[27] In the story of the healing of the leper, the verb that expresses Jesus' compassion – in Greek *splanchnistein* – has the same root as the word used to describe the Father's own feeling for us: because of his *tender compassion – splanchna –* he visited us from on high.[28] The Father is not unmoved by our situation and if anything he is even more eager than us to come to our help. The reason for these delays is a mystery and often a great cause of suffering for us. Faith, however, helps us to believe that God is only waiting for the best opportunity, for the *favourable time* to come to our help.[29] There is a delay God himself has

[26] Jn 3.16.
[27] Ps. 10.14.
[28] Lk. 1.78.
[29] 2 Cor 6.2.

to bear patiently, despite his eagerness: *I came to bring fire to the earth, and how I wish it were already kindled!*[30]

The good news, however, is that these delays can be affected by prayer. Bold, confident, persistent prayer can shorten these delays, can hasten God's help and intervention. This is why the Psalms brim with requests of this kind:

Be pleased, O Lord, to deliver me. O Lord, make haste to help me.[31]

O God, be not far from me. O my God, make haste to help me.[32]

Lord, I cry to you: make haste to help me, give ear to my voice when I cry to you.[33]

This is brought home in a surprising page of Mark's Gospel concerning the prayer of the Syrophoenician woman mentioned earlier *whose little daughter had an unclean spirit*. This woman heard about Jesus and she came and bowed down at his feet. *Now the woman was a Gentile, of Syrophoenician origin*. This means that she was a pagan. Up to that moment Jesus had deliberately confined his ministry to the Jews. In the Father's

[30] Lk. 12.49.
[31] Ps. 40.13,17.
[32] Ps. 71.12.
[33] Ps. 141.1.

plans for the salvation of humanity, the time to reach out to those who did not belong to the chosen people had not yet come. So when this woman begs Jesus to cast the demon out of her daughter, he gives her what sounds like a rather offensive and upsetting answer: *Let the children be fed first, for it is not fair to take the children's food and throw it to the dogs.* Why would someone like Jesus who came to give his life for all and did it because he loves each one of us – why would he reply like this, comparing the woman to a dog? Was it to test her determination? But would it not be sadistic to take advantage of a mother's pain on her child's account, even if it were for a good reason, the good of the woman herself?

Just as in most of Mark's Gospel, a lot takes place between the lines in this passage. Jesus recognizes immediately the exceptional character of this woman's faith and the woman is aware of this. There is some sort of chemistry between the two of them right from the beginning. Their dialogue resembles one of those innocent quarrels between two very close friends in which seemingly harsh words hide a deep and playful complicity. So the woman replies, *Sir, even the dogs under the table eat the children's crumbs.* Exactly the answer Jesus was waiting for, exactly the prayer or, even better, the *posture* he expected – the prayer, the posture, that allows him to grant whatever the woman asks for, making an exception to God's plans: '*For saying that, you may go – the demon has left your daughter.*'[34] For saying that, for praying in that way, for daring so much, for such an extraordinary trust, this woman had an effect on God's timing.

But we still need a final step to understand the necessity of perseverance, of boldness and trust in prayer, and why sometimes God seems to delay his intervention, to wait before he acts.

This time we are instructed by a blind beggar sitting by the roadside, Bartimaeus, whom Jesus met one day as he was leaving Jericho.[35] 'When Bartimaeus heard that Jesus of Nazareth was passing by he began to shout out and say, "Jesus, Son of David, have mercy on me!" Many sternly ordered him to be quiet, but he cried out even more loudly, "Son of David, have mercy on me!"'

This is how tenacious, dogged, daring we should be. Many people pretending to speak in Jesus' name, even members of the Church, who are supposed

[34] Mk 7.24–30.
[35] Mk 10.46–52.

to speak for him, will often discourage boldness in prayer, put limitations on the Lord's willingness and ability to come to our help, to forgive us, to listen to us. A Christian, however, always knows better and keeps hoping against hope.

And, indeed, Jesus stops, *stands still*, Mark tells us, and says, '*Call him here.*'

And they called the blind man, saying to him, 'Take heart; get up, he is calling you.' So, throwing off his cloak, Bartimaeus sprang up and came to Jesus. Jesus said to him, 'What do you want me to do for you?' The blind man said to him, 'My teacher, let me see again.' Jesus said to him, 'Go; your faith has made you well.' Immediately he regained his sight and followed him on the way.

Once again, Jesus knew this man needed him, so we are entitled to ask ourselves: why did he not go directly to him? This is what he did once with a paralytic who had been lying for thirty-eight years near the pool of Bethsaida and who had given up expecting anything. Jesus himself went to him and asked him, '*Do you want to get well?*'[36] In the case of Bartimaeus, if Jesus

---

[36] Jn 5.1–14.

seems to ignore him at first, if he does not prevent his disciples from trying to silence him, it must be for a reason. He wants to elicit this boldness and this perseverance in prayer from Bartimaeus and from all of us; he wants us to show staying power in our prayer and in our yearning. He wants our prayer to be lasting, our desire to be lasting, and to that effect he tells parables *about the need to keep praying and not to lose heart.*[37]

Bartimaeus, too, is healed by the same faith that we found in the leper, in the woman with the haemorrhage and in the Syrophoenician woman. The healing in all these cases is real, it concerns the body, it takes away a physical pain or impediment. But what prayer grants to these people is far more than a mere external, physical miracle. Somehow, the real miracle is this very prayer. The miracle is this perseverance, this boldness, this trust in prayer. This is why we have to persevere in prayer without ever losing heart, because already this persistence, this insistence, this enduring posture in the Father's presence, this effort to tune in with the prayer of the Spirit that goes on in our hearts : all this already *is* the miracle, already *is* the healing. This perseverance in prayer is that which purifies us, changes our heart, enlarges it and draws us nearer to God.

[37] Lk. 18.1.

THE WINGS OF A DOVE

How eagerly we long for rest! Not only physical rest,
but especially relief from the waves of worries and
anxieties about our loved ones, our work, the circumstances of our life. Our horizon is clouded, we have
no prospects for the future. We are overwhelmed by
grief or go through bouts of depression. We experience a painful break in a relationship, we have been
abandoned and all is misery and sadness. During these
times we might chance upon a Bible, open it at random
and be struck by one of the Psalms: 'And I say, Who
will give me wings like a dove? I would fly away and
be at rest; truly, I would flee far away; I would lodge
in the wilderness; I would hurry to find a shelter for
myself from the raging wind and tempest.'[1]

Flying far away, finding shelter and rest! Even if all
goes well and we are not in need of relief from a testing
situation, the normal wear and tear of life invariably
ends up leaving us homesick. We believe in God but

[1] Ps. 55.6–8.

we do not see him and often are tempted to think that he is absent. The existence of God and his active presence in our life will never be evident. However often we might have been blessed by the consolation faith brings to us, we share with the whole of humanity, believers and non-believers alike, the experience of the non-evidence of God. John's sentence at the beginning of his Gospel remains true for all of us: *Nobody has ever seen God* and nobody will ever see him as long as we are in this life.[2] This is what the allegory of the garden in the book of Genesis is meant to convey: we are away from the place where the Lord had initially established us, a place where he would *come for a walk every day at the time of the evening breeze*[3] to find his delight in our friendship.[4] Since the day we hid from his presence among the trees of the garden we have been unable to see him again. Faith has re-established the friendship, the relation; through faith we can somehow touch the Lord and be touched by him, but we are not yet back to the place where we can see him again.

This sentence from Psalm 55 speaks to us because we know that *as long as we are in this body we are away*

[2] Jn 1.18.
[3] Gen. 3.8.
[4] Cf. Wis. 7.14, 23 and Jn 15.15.

from the Lord and we walk by faith, not by sight.[5] Exiles long for their homeland. Augustine famously referred to this longing when he said that our heart is restless until it finds its rest in God.[6] There is a blessing in this longing, a particular kind of comfort attached to it. Jesus refers to it when he proclaims, *Blessed are those who mourn, for they will be comforted.*[7] This mourning echoes the tears of the people of Israel, who, when they were exiled from their homeland, *sat down by the rivers of Babylon and . . . wept when they remembered Zion;*[8] it also refers to the tears to be shed when our bridegroom is taken away from us.[9]

Prayer feeds on this longing, it is a mourning that is somehow also comforting, like the moaning of a dove.[10] 'In the day of my trouble I seek the Lord; in the night my hand is stretched out without wearying; my soul refuses to be comforted. I think of God, and I moan; I meditate, and my spirit faints.'[11] Scripture compares with doves those who pray, in order to indicate the Lord's desire for our trust and our love: *O my*

[5] Cor. 5.6–7.
[6] Augustine, *Confessions* 1.1.
[7] Mt. 5.4.
[8] Ps. 137.1.
[9] Mt. 9.15.
[10] Isa. 38.14.
[11] Ps. 77.2.

dove, in the clefts of the rock, in the covert of the cliff, let me see your face, let me hear your voice; for your voice is sweet, and your face is lovely.[12] Keener, much keener than our longing for the Lord is the Lord's longing for us: he wants to see our face, to hear our voice. In the Song of Songs the image of the dove reflects the love of the bridegroom for his bride and his delight in her. Because of our union with Christ, we too have become this dove when the Holy Spirit was poured in our heart,[13] the same Spirit who descended on Jesus under the form of a dove at his baptism to manifest that he was the beloved in whom the Father takes delight.[14]

Thanks to the Spirit, united with Christ, we too become like doves. This is a way of saying that our prayer is given wings – *O that I had wings like a dove!*[15] – the wings of our longing for the Lord and for his presence. We find fresh delight in friendship with God, we stop hiding from him, we join him when he wants to walk with us in the cool of the evening.

This cry therefore, *Who will give me wings like a dove?* means 'Who will teach me how to pray? Who will teach me to find rest and delight and consolation in

[12] Song 2.14.
[13] Rom. 5.5.
[14] Mt. 3.17.
[15] Ps. 55.6–8.

prayer?' We need to be given these wings if we want to go deeper into this loving friendship with the Lord, if we want prayer to be not only the occasional glance towards the Father (which is a good starting point and gives so much joy to him) but also a being led deeper into the 'secret' where the Father is attracting us, into this desert where he wants to speak to our heart: *I will now persuade her, and bring her into the wilderness, and speak tenderly to her.*[16]

At one point we are granted access to another dimension of prayer, one could say another level. Indeed, there are several dimensions of prayer just as there are several aspects to the life of faith.

We have seen that faith according to Mark consists in following Jesus, in sticking to him even when we do not understand him, even when he is walking on water and our faith falters:

Peter got out of the boat, started walking on the water, and came towards Jesus. But when he noticed the strong wind, he became frightened, and beginning to sink, he cried out, 'Lord, save me!' Jesus immediately reached out his hand and caught him, saying to him, 'You of little faith, why did you doubt?'[17]

[16] Hos. 2.14.
[17] Mt. 14.29–31.

As long as we stick to Jesus, and keep, like Peter, the reflex of turning to him, calling on him, appealing to him, even our little faith is not a problem, the raging waters will have no power over us, the Lord will always catch us: *he reached down from on high, he took me; he drew me out of mighty waters. He delivered me from my strong enemy and from those who hated me, for they were too mighty for me.*[18]

John in his Gospel compares faith not only to walking with Jesus, but especially to remaining with him, taking time to dwell with him. Jesus himself recommends this: 'Abide in me as I abide in you. Just as the branch cannot bear fruit by itself unless it abides in the vine, neither can you unless you abide in me . . . Those who abide in me and I in them bear much fruit, because apart from me you can do nothing.'[19]

This is what his disciples did from the beginning: *They came and saw where he was staying and they remained with him that day.*[20] This is how they were won over by him – they exposed themselves to his presence, listened to his word, saw his actions, ate and drank

[18] Ps. 18.16–17.
[19] Jn 15.4–5.
[20] Jn 1.39.

174

with him, enjoyed his friendliness, his gentleness, his consolation, and all this over time.

In the Lord's apparent absence, prayer is our way of abiding with him, and only enduring prayer can become a rest, a shelter, a source of relief, a desert where the Father can speak to our heart. The key to prayer is learning how to persevere in it, how to dwell in it and be at home there. Again, we are not talking about *prayers*, but about *prayer* – not an occasional activity, but something continuous, that we somehow put on and wear like clothing: *As God's chosen ones, holy and beloved, clothe yourselves with compassion, kindness, humility, meekness, and patience.*[21] How shall we nurture these feelings if not by dwelling close to the Father in prayer? Whenever Paul uses the language of clothing oneself in love, peace, faith, forgiveness, we can apply this to prayer:

> Clothe yourselves with love . . . let the peace of Christ rule in your hearts;[22] put on the armour of God . . . so that you may be able to withstand on that evil day, and having done everything, to stand firm . . . Take the shield of faith, with which you will be able to quench all the flaming arrows of the evil

[21] Col. 3.12.
[22] Col. 3.12,15.

one. Take the helmet of salvation, and the sword of
the Spirit, which is the word of God.[23]

Prayer is armour, shield and helmet in times of struggle, but also this gold-woven and many-coloured robe
in which the Spirit clothes us when we are led to the
king: 'The princess is decked in her chamber with
gold-woven robes; in many-coloured robes she is led
to the king; behind her the virgins, her companions,
follow. With joy and gladness they are led along as
they enter the palace of the king.'[24]

But how do we have access to a prayer of this kind, a
prayer that can last in this way, in which we can dwell,
that we can wear, that never leaves us? It cannot be
about increased focus or efforts. These can last only so
long and in any case we need to live, work, study, eat,
drink, sleep, make love, watch television, do sport, have
fun! How can we *pray without ceasing*,[25] *always and without growing weary*,[26] as Scripture recommends us to do?

The answer lies in the way we have approached the
Our Father as a *posture* rather than as a prayer. We have

[23] Eph. 6.11–17.
[24] Ps. 45.12–15.
[25] Thess. 5.17.
[26] Lk. 18.1.

seen that what is essential about the *Our Father* is not the words but the attitude it allows us to adopt in the presence of our Father, i.e. the trust, the assurance, the boldness of children who know that their Father wants to grant them everything.

To understand this better we need to pay greater attention to an apparent contradiction between Paul's two key sentences about prayer that have guided most of our reflection so far. As we have seen, on the one hand the Holy Spirit *in our heart constantly cries Abba! Father!*[27] and on the other hand he constantly *speaks for us with sighs too deep for words*.[28] We have seen that our prayer needs to tune in with this continuous prayer of the Holy Spirit in our heart, that our words should echo the words of the Spirit in our heart. This means that our prayer will not only have to learn how to echo the words *Abba! Father!* but also and especially these mysterious *sighs too deep for words*.

Indeed, the deeper we are led by the Spirit in prayer, the more those sighs will take over, not *our* sighs, but *the Spirit's sighs* in us. The deeper we are led by the Spirit in prayer, the more he takes over and all

[27] Gal. 4.6.
[28] Rom. 8.26.

we are asked to do is rest, leaving him to carry us on his wings. The real dove is the Spirit, his are the wings on which we can *fly away and be at rest . . . lodge in the wilderness and find a shelter*.[29]

The words of the *Our Father,* the words of the Psalms, as also the words we spontaneously say to the Lord with our lips or with our heart, are important as a way of expressing our trust in the Lord, our desire and our love for him. However, there are times when we do not need them any more. At one point silence takes over, not an empty silence, but a loving silence, a trusting silence, a desiring silence. We could say that sometimes when we pray we say words that help us to tune in with the Spirit who says *Abba Father* in our heart. At other times prayer becomes a tuning in with this wordless sighing of the Spirit, and then we become like a lamp that burns in the presence of the Lord and that very burning is our prayer.

We reach here what Christian spiritual tradition has often referred to as 'contemplative' prayer. Talk about contemplation is ambivalent because it has often been seen as a way of getting access to a special perception of God beyond Christ, beyond Scripture, beyond the

[29] Ps. 55.6–8.

Church. In this meaning it is dangerous and misleading because it is just a more refined form of idolatry: a way of gaining access to a deeper stream of energy, a deeper level of consciousness, which ultimately (whether we are aware of this or not, and whether we acknowledge it or not) is meant to give us greater self-control, greater power. A very dangerous temptation indeed because it presents itself disguised as *an angel of light*.[30]

But there is an authentic Christian way of approaching this aspect of prayer, which simply corresponds to what we have seen about the *Our Father* being not one of the prayers, but the key to *prayer*, to the worship in spirit and truth that Jesus has taught us, to the *posture* we are invited to embrace in the presence of the Father. Far from leading us beyond Christ, the Scripture or the Church, an authentic *contemplative prayer* flourishes only when, through trust, desire and love, we remain in Christ and Christ remains in us[31] and when we really *receive the word of God not as a human word but for what it really is, God's word, which is at work in those who believe*.[32]

[30] Cor. 11.14.
[31] Jn 15.4.
[32] Thess. 2.13.

A WHISPER

Just as he declares *it is not I who live, but it is Christ who lives in me*,[1] so Paul also implies that 'It is not I who pray, but the Spirit who prays in me', since the fundamental law of prayer for him is that *We do not know how to pray.*[2] Spiritual authors have often stressed the extent to which, far from depending on increased focus and efforts or cleverer methods, progress in prayer results from 'letting go', from allowing God to take over. To express the same idea, the analogy we have used so far has been that of tuning in to the prayer of the Spirit which always goes on in our heart.

The challenge here is perceiving this ongoing prayer of the Spirit in us as God's call to join it. Another way of saying the same thing is that we need to learn how to recognize God's presence and action in our lives. Two episodes of the Old Testament offer vivid illustrations of this challenge and of the ways in which we should meet it.

[1] Gal. 2.20.
[2] Rom. 8.26.

Let us look first at the endearing young prophet Samuel,[3] who was *serving to the Lord under* the priest Eli at a time when not only the people but also the priests were not very keen on hearing the word of the Lord. This young boy used to lie down in the temple and was full of zeal for the Lord, eager to serve and to obey. This very eagerness, however, misleads him when the Lord comes to visit him. Three times the Lord calls him – *Samuel, Samuel* – but each time the boy runs to Eli instead, thinking that the priest needs him. The problem was that *Samuel did not yet know the Lord, and the word of the Lord had not yet been revealed to him.*[4]

The priest, however, at one point understood that Samuel was not just having a bad dream, but that it was the Lord wanting to talk to the boy. Even though he was a negligent priest using religion for his own advantage (later in the book we see him punished for this),[5] Eli had some experience of the way the Lord acts and was still able to recognize it. There is a distinctive character of God, a typical way in which he intervenes in history. He tends to have a predilection for people nobody would think of: shepherds like

[3] Cf. 1 Sam. 3.
[4] Sam. 3.7.
[5] Sam. 4.18.

Moses or later David, young people. Also, he is a God who never gives up on us. If we do not welcome him or do not recognize him the first time, he keeps calling and knocking at our door until we open: 'Listen! I am standing at the door, knocking; if you hear my voice and open the door, I will come in to you and eat with you, and you with me.'[6]

Before being an invitation addressed to us, Jesus' sentence, *Ask, and it will be given to you; search, and you will find; knock, and the door will be opened for you,*[7] is a description of the way God acts with us. It is God who perseveres in asking, knocking and searching for us. The whole history of salvation can be read as a version of the parable of the prodigal son in which the Father not only welcomes us when we come back to him, but travels himself to the far country in search of us, and when he finds us, he does not force us, but first comforts us in our loneliness and despair; only then does he try to win us over, to *persuade us*, by speaking kindly to our heart.[8]

God could have made himself known from the beginning to Samuel with signs and miracles, as he

[6] Rev. 3.20.
[7] Lk. 11.9.
[8] Cf. Hos. 2.14.

often did in the history of salvation when addressing his people. His real style, however, is different; it is gentle, gently persistent, so that we remain free to welcome him and listen to him.

The priest Eli must have recognized, by the persistence of the call and by its gentleness, that this was the Lord, so he says to Samuel: *Go, lie down; and if he calls you, you shall say, 'Speak, Lord, for your servant is listening.'* And indeed the Lord comes yet another time and he *calls as before, 'Samuel! Samuel!' And Samuel said, 'Speak, for your servant is listening.'*[9]

This is how Samuel discovers God's presence. He already lived in the temple, he was even accustomed to lie down by the ark of the covenant which was held to be the place of God's presence. But what follows is an anticipation of Jesus' words to the Samaritan woman: 'The hour is coming when you will worship the Father neither on this mountain nor in Jerusalem . . . when the true worshippers will worship the Father in spirit and truth, for the Father seeks such as these to worship him.'[10] God's presence is not to be sought in churches or shrines, on mountains or in deserts. This search for sacred places

[9] Sam. 3.9–10.
[10] Jn 4.21ff.

is yet another illusion, another manifestation of our entrenched paganism, the idolatry we shall never overcome once and for all.

Since the moment we left the garden and fled from the Lord's presence, or thought we had – since that moment the Lord has followed us and taken care of us. Already in the book of Genesis we have a touching image that expresses this truth. He does not let us go before having made *garments of skin to clothe us*.[11] He keeps telling us that he is the *God with us*,[12] the God who never leaves our side, wherever we might get lost:

> Where can I go from your spirit? Or where can I flee from your presence? If I ascend to heaven, you are there; if I make my bed in Sheol, you are there. If I take the wings of the morning and settle at the furthest limits of the sea, even there your hand shall lead me, and your right hand shall hold me fast. If I say, 'Surely the darkness shall cover me, and the light around me become night', even the darkness is not dark to you; the night is as bright as the day, for darkness is as light to you.[13]

[11] Gen. 3.21.
[12] Cf. Deut. 6.15.
[13] Ps. 139.7–12

Prayer is discovering this presence of the Lord beside us and within us wherever we are. Words, prayers, special places may help, but they are secondary and ultimately useless if we do not learn how to welcome this presence and to walk beside the Lord just as he walks with us.

There is yet more to be learnt from another Old Testament figure, a formidable character, a man of fire, devoured by the zeal of God: the prophet Elijah. When we meet him, he has already been speaking in the Lord's name for a long while, and often been the instrument of God's action. He was like many Christians or ministers in our churches today who are so busy doing things for the Lord and acting in his name that they never have the time, the energy or simply the patience to just stay put, abiding in the Lord's presence, or going *to a place where they can rest by the Lord for a little while*.[14]

Elijah had been consumed by his zeal and reached a point of discouragement and exhaustion; he was under threat and feared for his life. So he went a day's journey into the wilderness, sat down under a solitary broom tree and asked that he might die: 'It is enough;

[14] Mk 6.31.

now, O Lord, take away my life, for I am no better than my ancestors.'[15]

As is often the case, however, it is precisely at this juncture in life, when crisis or failure has made us more vulnerable, when we finally sit down and pause for a moment, that we discover God's presence at our side in an entirely new and comforting way. The bread and water Elijah suddenly finds beside him are the symbol of the consolation that the presence of the Lord brings to us, of the new energies he awakens in us, of the renewed warmth with which he fills our hearts.

But this is not enough. As for Samuel earlier, so for Elijah it is time to be introduced into this worship in spirit and truth which the Father seeks, time to learn how to really listen to the voice of the Lord. And here we come to one of the most evocative pages of the Old Testament. Elijah climbs a mountain and waits for the Lord to manifest himself.

Now there was a great wind, so strong that it was splitting mountains and breaking rocks in pieces before the Lord, but the Lord was not in the wind; and after the wind an earthquake, but the Lord was not in the earthquake; and after the earthquake a fire, but the Lord was not in the fire; and after the

[15] Kgs 19.4.

fire a sound of sheer silence. When Elijah heard it, he wrapped his face in his mantle and went out and stood at the entrance of the cave.[16]

Translators here have shown a lot of imagination: what Elijah heard was a 'gentle whisper', a 'soft whisper', a 'gentle blowing', a 'still small voice', a 'quiet whispering voice', a 'whistling of a gentle air', 'the sound of sheer silence'. The main idea is that it was not something imposing or spectacular. On the contrary, it was something we can easily miss unless we pay attention, unless we want to hear it, unless we ourselves are silent.

We are so often busy standing and ministering in our churches, heaping up phrases, thinking we will be heard by the Lord because of our many words,[17] that we miss the crucial moment in our prayer when we are invited to rest for a while, to sit and be silent, to simply dwell and continue in God's presence and listen. This silence we are so afraid of might not be empty after all; it might have a sound, it might be filled with God's presence.

[16] Kgs 19.11–13.
[17] Mt. 6.5ff.

What does it take finally to listen to God's whisper? It is the greatest challenge in our life of prayer, the decisive test of the real eagerness of our desire, of the authenticity of our faith and of our love for the Lord.

We are not asked to empty ourselves nor to gain access to a higher level of self-awareness. It is not about us. Even though the movement is indeed directed inwardly, it is about forgetting ourselves for a little while and paying attention to the Lord instead. It is the deepening of a friendship. It is often said that a friendship is real when two friends can spend time silently together without the least embarrassment, feeling instead that this connects them at a deeper level. It is about having access to a trust, a desire and a love so deep, so intense, so free that words can no longer express what they feel. Such trust, such desire and such love can only express themselves through *sighs too deep for words*.

THE SHEPHERD'S WHISTLE

So the question is this: how do we become aware of God's presence, how do we recognize it? We are talking about an entirely unique and special presence. The presence of the Lord whom *nobody has ever seen*,[1] in whom *we live and move and have our being*,[2] who *surrounds his people*[3] and each one of us – *You surround me – before me and behind me. You lay your hand on me*[4] – whose love constantly urges us on.[5] We should never forget that when we talk about the presence of God we are always using images, metaphors. He cannot be located anywhere, he is everywhere or rather we are in him.

And yet the New Testament favours images that locate this presence within us. We have several times already met key sentences by Paul about prayer that invite us to look for God's presence inside us: in us the Spirit prays and sighs,[6] he dwells in us as

[1] Jn 1.18.
[2] Acts 17.28.
[3] Ps. 125.2.
[4] Ps. 139.5.
[5] Cor. 5.14.
[6] Gal. 4.6 and Rom. 8.26.

in a temple,[7] Christ lives in us.[8] We also saw Jesus himself declaring in the Gospel of John, *I abide in you*,[9] adding that he and the Father come in and make their home in us.[10] Christian spiritual tradition about prayer has consistently done the same and invited Christians to look for God inside themselves, to dwell with him by withdrawing within themselves. The similarity of the language and images adopted by Christian authors across vastly different spiritual traditions and periods concerning this inward movement is startling.

Here, for example, is Bernard of Clairvaux, writing in the twelfth-century Western monastic tradition, and describing in one of his sermons[11] how we can discern God's presence within us. He admits that the Lord has come to him, but in a mysterious way:

> I admit that the Word has also come to me and has done so many times. But although he has come to me, I have never been conscious of the moment of his coming. I perceived his presence, I remembered afterwards that he had been with me; sometimes I

---

[7] Cor. 6.19.
[8] Gal. 2.20.
[9] Jn 15.4.
[10] Jn 14.23.
[11] Bernard of Clairvaux, *On the Song of Songs*, Sermon 74, II.5.

had a presentiment that he would come, but I was
never conscious of his coming or his going.

To describe the moment of prayer when we become
aware of God's presence Bernard uses the image of
a visit: it is as if God had come to us, had dwelt in
us for a while in a special way. And to explain the
challenge concerning the way in which we discover
this presence Bernard expands the image (and let
us remember it is just an image, like all the others
used to the same effect) by comparing it to someone
coming to our home whom we only noticed once he
was already there:

> Where he comes from when he visits my soul, and
> where he goes, and by what means he enters and
> goes out, I admit that I do not know even now; as
> John says: *You do not know where he comes from or where
> he goes.*[12] There is nothing strange in this, for of him
> was it said, *Your footsteps will not be known.*[13] . . . How
> then did he enter? Perhaps he did not enter because
> he does not come from outside? He is not one of
> the things which exist outside us. Yet he does not
> come from within me, for he is good, and I know
> that there is no good in me. I have ascended to the

[12] Jn 3.8.
[13] Ps. 77.19.

193

highest in me, and look! the word is towering above that. In my curiosity I have descended to explore my lowest depths, yet I found him even deeper. If I looked outside myself, I saw him stretching beyond the furthest I could see; and if I looked within, he was yet further within. Then I knew the truth of what I had read, *In him we live and move and have our being.*[14] And blessed is the man in whom he has his being, who lives for him and is moved by him.

The main interest of this text lies in the way that Bernard explains how he finally recognized that it was the Lord. This is a real riddle: if God's presence in us is so tenuous, so mysterious, if we can so easily miss it, how can we be sure that we are not just deluding ourselves? When we think that we recognize him, how do we know it is not just our imagination? Bernard first formulates the question: 'You ask then how I knew he was present, when his ways can in no way be traced?' His answer focuses on the effects of this presence on him:

> God is life and power and so, as soon as he enters in me, he awakens my slumbering soul; he stirs and soothes and pierces my heart, for before it was hard

[14] Acts 17.28.

as stone, and diseased . . . When the bridegroom, the Word, came to me, he never made known his coming by any signs, not by sight, not by sound, not by touch. It was not by any movement of his that I recognized his coming; it was not by any of my senses that I perceived he had penetrated to the depths of my being. *Only by the movement of my heart, as I have told you, did I perceive his presence.*

This is a lovely sentence: we perceive the presence of the Lord 'by the movement of our heart'. This echoes the teaching of the New Testament about the action of the Holy Spirit in us. He is the *comforter*,[15] he *consoles us*,[16] so that one of the signs that the Lord is present is the mysterious peace that floods the heart. Paul lists peace among the fruits of the Holy Spirit together with love, joy, patience and perseverance.[17] There is a distinctive brand of peace and of joy which only God can give, the joy promised by Christ: *I have said these things to you so that my joy may be in you, and that your joy may be complete.*[18] Once tasted, this peace and this joy are unmistakeable and they become the

[15] Jn 14.26.
[16] Cor. 1.4.
[17] Gal. 5.22–23.
[18] Jn 15.11.

signs that the Lord is present to us or rather that we are more present to him in our prayer.

It is striking to find an analogous explanation from Theophan the Recluse (1815–94), a spiritual author belonging to a very different tradition, who lived in Russia as a hermit most of his life. He says this:

> Divine action is not something material: it is invisible, inaudible, unexpected, unimaginable, and inexplicable by any analogy taken from this world. Its advent and its working within us are a mystery . . . Little by little, divine action grants to man increased attention and contrition of the heart in prayer.[19]

Theophan, too, emphasizes the mysterious character of God's presence and the fact that it can be discerned by its effects: it increases our attention on God and our longing for him. The following section of his text, however, adopts a more psychological approach to discerning God's presence, i.e. an approach consisting in paying attention not only to what we feel about God (increased trust or desire, love, peace, joy, longing) but also to the effects of this presence on our psyche: 'Having prepared the vessel

[19] Chariton of Valamo, *The Art of Prayer: An Orthodox Anthology*, trans. E. Dakloubovsky and E. Palmer (London: Faber and Faber, 1997), 147f.

in this manner, it touches the severed parts suddenly, unexpectedly, immaterially, and they become united in one.'[20]

From the fifteenth century onwards, Christian spirituality has developed an increasing fascination for the psychological effects of God's presence on us in prayer. Countless treatises of spirituality were written on these topics, especially in the nineteenth and early twentieth century, and when we read them today we cannot avoid finding them rather esoteric. Even when we talk about prayer we fall prey to our fundamental narcissism and end up talking about ourselves instead of God.

It is true, however, that when we are introduced into this dimension of prayer something changes in us. The usual unruliness of our thoughts and imagination wanes for a while, not as a result of increased focus on our part, but because of something that captures us and our attention. The moment we tune in with the prayer of the Holy Spirit within, the moment we let him take over, the experience of prayer changes dramatically. Focusing is no longer a problem. Unruly thoughts, memories, worries either disappear or

[20] Chariton of Valamo, *The Art of Prayer*, 148.

lose their power to distract. Theophan attributes this sudden change of atmosphere in prayer to God 'touching' our heart and thus unifying it.

Although using different images, the sixteenth-century author Teresa of Avila describes the same experience in her well-known treatise *The Interior Castle,* in which she uses the image of a castle with many halls to describe progress in the life of prayer. Each of these halls corresponds to a new level of awareness of God's presence, and the decisive moment we are describing in this chapter corresponds to her fourth hall (or 'mansion').

First, Teresa stresses that access to this deeper level of awareness of God's presence is not something that results from greater knowledge, from the sharpening of our understanding or of our senses: 'Do not fancy you can gain it by thinking of God dwelling within you, or by imagining Him as present in your soul . . . for it is founded on the fact that God resides within us.' This is a gift from God, something that we only have to welcome and acknowledge:

Sometimes, before we have begun to think of God, we find ourselves within the castle. I know not by what means we entered, nor how we heard the shepherd's whistle; the ears perceived no sound but the soul is keenly conscious of a delicious sense of recollection experienced by those who enjoy this favour, which I cannot describe more clearly.

Just as sheep immediately gather around the shepherd when they hear the sound of his whistle, so this increased faith, desire and love for God resulting from a deeper awareness of his presence somehow pull together and unify our mind and our heart:

The soul is then like a tortoise or sea-urchin, which retreats into itself . . . but these creatures can withdraw into themselves at will, while here it is not in our power to retire into ourselves, unless God gives us the grace . . . Some books advise that as a preparation for hearing what our Lord may say to us we should keep our minds at rest, waiting to see what he will work in our souls. But unless His Majesty has begun to suspend our faculties, I cannot understand how we are to stop thinking, without doing ourselves more harm than good.

We could quote numerous other authors, from very different spiritual traditions, who describe the same experience. It is striking to see that without having read each other's writings or even, in some cases, been aware of the others' existence, they use very similar images to describe their experience of prayer. They insist especially on one point, namely that we are somehow 'taken' by this prayer, that we are led by it more than we lead it. Here again the nineteenth-century Russian hermit Theophan:

> The spirit of prayer comes upon man and drives him into the depths of the heart, as if he were taken by the hand and forcibly led from one room to another. The soul is here taken captive by an invading force, and is kept willingly within, as long as this over-whelming power of prayer still holds sway over it.[21]

Only when we see prayer in this way can we make sense of Paul's encouragement to *pray without ceasing*.[22] He is not describing something resulting from super-human self-control, but simply a silently burning faith, desire, love and longing for God, in unison with the prayer of the Holy Spirit that goes on constantly in our heart. Remaining longer in this state of prayer happens of itself; it can be said that 'it is prayer itself that expands its domain'.[23]

---

[21] Chariton of Valamo, *The Art of Prayer*, 65.
[22] Thess. 5.17.
[23] Chariton of Valamo, *The Art of Prayer*, 83.

AFRAID OF DISAPPOINTMENT

Where have we lost our prayer? What has withered, tired, drained it? Why has it become so formal, so poor, little more than a habit? A few minutes at most – an idle interval reluctantly pulled out of my day. A few minutes I skip, waste, leave out on the slightest pretext. A few minutes spent fighting against sleep, boredom, projects, concerns, memories and the crowd of thoughts suddenly pressing into my head and my heart as soon as I try to pray.

Where have we lost our prayer? How have the wings that allow us to fly got broken? *To you, O Lord, I lift up my soul.* How can we rise to the Lord if our foot is caught in the snare of the fowler?[1]

We pray badly, we pray little, we pray to quieten our conscience, we pray only when and as long as we need to, and fall back soon into our usual lassitude. We lack faith. Our desire is worn out. Our lamps are drained of oil. Our hope is withered. Most of all, we have lost the way to *true* prayer, to *authentic* prayer.

[1] Ps. 25.1, 15.

We never acknowledge enough the poverty of our prayer, our neglect, our carelessness. We keep feeling guilty about it and try to make new resolutions: 'Now I want to pray more and better', without success. Until we dare to raise a question: is it really our fault? Or, is it *just* our fault? We ask, seek, knock ineptly, that's for sure – but the Lord does not seem to respond any better. We are, indeed, often absent from our hearts and distracted in our minds, but the Lord too remains wrapped in the same impenetrable silence, always invisible, always out of reach:

God, though to Thee our psalm we raise
No answering voice comes from the skies;
To Thee the trembling sinner prays
But no forgiving voice replies;
Our prayer seems lost in desert ways,
Our hymn in the vast silence dies.[2]

No one has ever seen God,[3] no voice comes down from heaven. Silence is the Lord's dwelling-place: we do not see him, we do not hear him and even when we feel something, how can we be sure that it is really

[2] Gerard Manley Hopkins, '*Nondum*', in *La Freschezza più cara. Poesie scelte*, ed. Antonio Spadaro (Milano: Rizzoli, 2008), 46.
[3] Jn 1.18.

God and not an illusion? How many other voices submerge us, deafen us, confuse us: ambitions, qualms, anxieties, jealousies, fears, guilt.

We should not idealize prayer. It is a difficult art, a painstaking skill, an uneven path, mostly uphill, and in the end authentic prayer comes to us only as a gift. The Psalmist does not idealize prayer. Indeed, he starts by saying, *To you, O Lord, I lift up my soul*, but immediately he adds: *Let me not be disappointed*. And he repeats, *Guard my life and rescue me, Let me not be disappointed, for I take refuge in you.*[4]

He says, he repeats: *Let me not be disappointed.* The first step into prayer is acknowledging our fear of being disappointed, of being ashamed – acknowledging our disappointment.

Prayer disappoints us. The Church too disappoints us: every day the same sad show of mediocrity and meanness, of flattery, sometimes even of unbearable prostitution. We are disappointed not only with prayer, not only with the Church, but also with ourselves: think of all the enthusiasm with which we gave ourselves to the Lord and how we end up tired, negligent, internally divided, heavy, hungry, anxious: *The troubles of my*

[4] Ps. 25.1–2, 20.

heart have multiplied; free me from my anguish. Look upon my affliction and my distress and take away all my sins.[5]

The most authentic prayer, then, is this: *Let me not be disappointed*! 'May my hope remain alive!' 'May my enthusiasm not die!' 'May cynicism, scepticism, disillusionment not win over me!'

Do we not meet this cynicism, this indifference, this resignation all around us every day? How many of our Christian brothers and sisters have succumbed to them? How many of our pastors have given up? And we too, are we not dismayed to discover the seeds of these feelings in our own hearts? We become disillusioned, resigned, cold, indifferent, and slowly, inexorably, cynical too.

Prayer disappoints me. The Church disappoints me. I'm disappointed with myself.

Yet we have not hit bottom. The Psalmist goes further. He is much bolder than we are. He is unable to keep to himself a still deeper anxiety: he fears being disappointed not just by prayer, not just by the Church, not just by himself. Greater still is his fear of being disappointed in and by God. To the Lord he shouts: *Let me not be disappointed*; to him he repeats a second time: *Let me not be disappointed*.

[5] Ps. 25.17–18.

'I have not put hope in myself, O Lord, nor have I trusted my own strength. I have not put my hope in people – not even in people of the Church. In you I have put my hope, to you I shout, *Let me not be disappointed*.'

If we do not want to get lost, to dry up, to sink into disillusionment, coldness and resignation, then our prayer needs to be authentic. Piety is not enough. Niceness does not work when we pray! We need to find a deeper voice, a more genuine yearning in our hearts. We need to let its deepest groans and shouts rise to the surface: *My heart and my flesh cry out for the living God.*[6]

Thus, the doorway into prayer can indeed be this beautiful sentence: *To you, O Lord, I lift up my soul.* But only the remaining part of Psalm 25 unveils the real identity of this soul that rises to God, that seeks a path to God through prayer: it is a soul fully aware of its weight, a soul that does not run away from the body, that does not flee from the world or try to evade history. It is the biblical soul: the breath that dwells in the flesh, that moves the bones, that breathes life into clay. Not an agile, a lightweight breath, but a tangle of anguish, of sorrow, of tiredness, always threatened by the ghost of disappointment.

[6] Ps. 84.2.

Far too spiritual, our prayer is asphyxiated by good manners. If I do not allow my fears to pray, if I do not allow my anger and my flesh to pray, if I do not give voice to my disappointment and to my anxiety, how can my prayer be true, how can it be *human*, how can it be a true expression of faith, of trust and of hope in God?

If the Psalmist dares to ask the Lord not to let him down, if he dares to express his fear of being disappointed by the Lord, it is not because he doubts the Lord. He dares, he knows he can dare, because he fully trusts him: *In you I trust, O my God. Let me not be disappointed*; and again: *Let me not be disappointed, for I take refuge in you.*

True faith, true trust, can be recognized in this attitude. This is the land of authentic prayer, a prayer that does not wear out, a prayer that never dies, a prayer that knows it can dare and is not afraid of shouting *Do not disappoint me, O Lord*! 'Do not let indifference and coldness overrun me! May I not be overwhelmed by my enemies: cynicism, disillusionment, resignation!'

In this way we will be granted access to a prayer that grows more authentic, more human, more confident, because it becomes more daring. In this way we are granted access to a prayer in which we might even learn to persevere.

THESE WORDS I COULD
NOT SAY

Among the prayers I am fond of I love to include 'Jesus to a Child', George Michael's 1994 song dedicated to his lover Anselmo Feleppa whom he met in Rio de Janeiro in 1991. Anselmo died in 1993 from an AIDS-related brain haemorrhage. After grieving for almost two years, in just an hour George Michael wrote a song that was not just a hit at the time but carries on speaking to the hearts of people and has become part of that body of poems we cherish as our enduring store of consolation and meaning.

What makes it a prayer is not its title. 'Jesus to a Child' is a simple comparison meant to evoke the gentlest possible way of looking at a person: *You smiled at me like Jesus to a child*. We might be tempted to flesh out this comparison, to go to the Gospels and look at the times Jesus was with children, at what he said about them or to them and imagine what kind of smile might have been on his face on these occasions. But this would force the meaning of the song. What matters in this comparison is the smile. Eyes are in the initial sentences of the first two verses: *kindness in your eyes . . . sadness in my eyes*. Through the eyes a life-giving smile guesses the sadness, hears the cry, sees the pain and the tears, and pours kindness on a *loveless and cold* heart. The unspoken cry for help – *no one guessed, well no one tried* – was met by the prevenient, unexpected blessing of understanding – *I guess you heard me cry* – and by a winning, compassionate love. That instant sealed the bond.

Prayer has its 'laws', it works in a certain way, it takes certain paths. Most of these are the same as in friendship and love, most are as paradoxical as the laws and the paths of friendship and love. The first of these laws is that *we do not know how to pray*, not only initially but always, because prayer is free. However often we may have prayed, we are never guaranteed that it will happen again. Prayer only happens when I experience a connection, a double connection, both with the deepest part of my heart and with the deepest 'thing out there', whatever it might be. Most of the time, access to this deepest part of my heart is barred and this deepest thing out there, call it destiny or fate or nature, is something I sense or fear and prefer to ignore. Even just to think of it makes me uncomfortable. But then life snatches me out of this precarious compromise, shakes me to the core, and I am forced to probe in both directions, both inside me and out there, in a desperate search for meaning. It took eighteen months of grief, pain and tears for George Michael finally to experience this connection: *but now I know . . . I can say . . .*

Heaven sent and heaven stole: the smile that had brought him consolation, the love he had waited for *all those years, just when it began*, was taken away. Pain and tears, *I thought I would never feel the same*. Once again he is left *loveless and cold*. Coldness swallows us when to loss and loneliness is added the absurdity and meaninglessness of it all – and guilt: what can I have done to deserve this? What monstrous thing out there can send and then steal in this way, grant you incommensurable warmth one moment only to plunge you again in darkness and coldness with nowhere to go, nobody to appeal to, only loss and pain? And a pain which I have to cling to because it is the only remaining connection with the person I loved, the only way he still remains alive somewhere in me, the only way I can still be faithful to him, faithful to this love. *I thought I'd never feel the same about anyone or anything again.*

Until, at one point, this connection happens. I am granted access to this deepest part of me and I discover that love, that my lover, still is alive, that the treasure of warmth I received is preserved there intact, beating – it had been waiting for me, waiting for the loss and grief to do their job. This newly discovered treasure of inner warmth can lead me to another level of reality, to another way of looking at life, at me, at the world, so that I can finally reconcile myself with them. Then I discover that that *last breath* which stole my love from me, which I thought was the end of it and of my life, had in fact *saved my soul*. Then these *cold, cold nights* are not endless any more because *the lover that you miss will come to you . . . the lover that you kissed will comfort you.*

You have been loved . . . you know it holds such bliss . . . you know that it exists . . . and you say it: *I can still say . . .* Say it, but why? And to whom? It is a message for everyone: I am still alive, even more alive than before. Grief is not the only way to be faithful to my love, to keep him alive. I do not need to keep him alive by pain and tears. He *is* alive, because his love in me is alive, because *every single memory has become a part of me.* The words that had escaped me until now, I can now sing: *when you find a love, when you know that it exists . . .* he does not die, he is alive in me and wants me to be alive for him, for us: *And the love we would have made I'll make it for two.*

Access to the deepest part of myself, to this *soul* saved by my lover's *last breath*, also gives me the strength and the courage to confront, to challenge, the thing out there, whether it is destiny, or fate, or nature – whether benevolent of cynical or just indifferent to my life – I can challenge this *heaven* that *sent* only to cruelly *steal* from me:

> 'Hey, thing out there, I do not get you! But whether you care about this or not, whether you can listen to me or not, well *now I know* and can *still say*: I am alive, and my lover is alive in me, I can still sing, my love has not been crushed, I can now *make it for two*. He *will always be my love, always by my side*. I still miss him, but his breath is with me, and so is that smile that was *jesus to a child*.'

When I know this thing I have to say it, sing it. When I have experienced this connection I know it is not only for me, it has to become a poem and a message – and more than this, it has to become a *prayer*. A poem might say something deep but will not always be life-giving. A message can convey a truth, but this truth can be desperate and cynical. Prayer alone will always bring comfort and hope: it *will comfort you when there is no hope in sight*. Only through prayer *the lover that you miss will come to you on those cold, cold nights*.

If you have understood anything about prayer, if you have ever been given the blessing of erupting in the kind of prayer George Michael experienced as the outcome of all his grief, then you will acquire new eyes. You will become able to see prayer everywhere and often where you least expect to find it. More importantly, you will become deeply aware that you do not know how to pray, you never know how to pray and that you are never better at it than anybody else, whether believer or non-believer, whether a good or a bad person, whatever his or her religion, faith, sexual orientation, life-choice. Indeed the fundamental law of prayer – that we do not know how to pray – is only the tails side of the coin. The heads side is that prayer is *free*. No religion owns it because no religion owns God, no religion can guarantee access to God or, for that matter, to meaning and comfort and hope. Meaning, comfort and hope are a gift, a *grace*, and they reach us when we least expect it, from inside, like a sudden refreshing breeze: *you hear its sound but you do not know where it comes from or where it goes*.[1]

[1] Jn 3.8.

SAY IT TO GOD

Searching for prayer means learning how to listen to
the deepest voice within us, discerning our innermost
yearning, looking for our core desire. It is a journey
that teaches us what we really want or rather that puts
us *in touch* with it. We think we know what we want
but we spend most of our lives chasing after whims
that leave us exhausted and empty-handed.

While initially inviting us to enter into ourselves,
prayer eventually leads us beyond ourselves, not
because our concerns become irrelevant or we disappear, but because we truly find ourselves only when
we are introduced into a personal relationship. Prayer
is not about unveiling an impersonal source of our
being, nor about gaining access to some sort of basic
cosmic energy, nor about diving into a greater whole.
Prayer is meeting the Father's eyes and discovering
that he loves us, cares for us and journeys at our side.
When we meet this love, when we *feel* it, then we are
given new eyes, a new heart and new strength – then
we are given wings. Life will never be the same again.

Not that pain, worry, sin, selfishness, shame, guilt, magically disappear. Not that we lose our solidarity with all our brothers and sisters who do not pray or do not believe. On the contrary, authentic prayer makes us more compassionate: we start feeling not only our pain but the pain of our brothers and sisters as well, we start perceiving the inward groans of humanity and even of the whole of creation.[1] What changes, however, is that these groans, this pain, these worries, this shame, this guilt, become prayer, feed prayer so that love and hope are inexplicably infused into them and they lose their bitterness, their ability to hurt us, to trouble us: *in hope we were saved and when we hope we* become able to *wait with patience, because all things work together for good for those who experience God's love* in prayer.[2]

A monk once told me this: 'Whenever I have a bitterness in my heart, I put it between me and God in prayer until he changes it into sweetness.' Prayer removes the poison of bitterness from our hearts. Prayer comforts us, consoles us – and heaven knows how much, how urgently, how desperately we need to be comforted. We know that we have met the real

[1] Rom. 8.19–23.
[2] Rom. 8.25, 28.

214

God, the Father, only when prayer starts bringing us this consolation: 'Blessed be the Father of mercies and the God of all consolation, who consoles us in all our afflictions, so that we may be able to console those who are in any affliction with the consolation with which we ourselves are consoled by God.'[3]

Each time thinking of God causes us to fear, makes us feel guilty, leaves us lonely and cold, it means that what we have just met is one of our projections of God, one of our heartless idols, but certainly not the Father, not *this* Father.

Christian churches have their rules, they have to say what is right and what is wrong. Society does the same. So do our families and even our friends. And when we are wrong in their eyes – in the eyes of our family, friends, society, or church – we feel unworthy to be loved and forgiven, however much we might affect indifference towards them, whether they are right or wrong (and most of the time they are a bit of both). We often do not know ourselves whether we are right or wrong, why we do what we do. We mess up a lot . . .: *I do not understand my own actions. For I do not do what I want, but I do the very things I hate.*[4]

[3] Cor. 1.3–4.
[4] Rom. 7.15.

But society, churches, families and friends, too, mess up a lot. Few things awaken Jesus' anger more than the attitude of those who *tie up heavy burdens, hard to bear, and lay them on the shoulders of others, but they themselves are unwilling to lift a finger to move them.*[5]

In the end the source of authentic peace and truth will have to be looked for within. The real source of certainty as well. The moment comes when we are invited to reclaim our freedom – not any freedom, but the freedom of the children of God, and take our responsibility: *For freedom Christ has set us free!*[6]

When we really meet the Father, when we are regenerated by his love, by his comfort and by his hope, it is as if oil is poured on our wounds. This oil, this anointing, both comforts and teaches us, it instructs us from within, it sharpens our instincts, gives us a new ability to discern, to tell what comes from God and what doesn't: 'As for you, the anointing that you received from him abides in you, and so you do not need anyone to teach you. But as his anointing teaches you about all things, and is true and is not a lie, and just as it has taught you, abide in him.'[7]

[5] Mt. 23.4.
[6] Gal. 5.1.
[7] Jn 2.27.

Jesus says two things about the Spirit of the Father, the Spirit that is his gift to us and that he has sent into our hearts. He says that this Spirit will introduce us into the whole truth[8] – about God, about ourselves and about the world. He says too that this Spirit will be our sure source of comfort and consolation, as shown by his name of *Comforter*.[9] This gives us a fundamental criterion for discerning God's truth among all other claims, even those made in God's name and pretending to be his truth. We know that we are dealing with God's truth when it brings us comfort and consolation, when it dispels guilt, shame, anxiety and fear and fills us with peace, joy and love.

Only those who pray, those who dwell in the Father and are in tune with the Spirit, can have this experience, can have access to this truth.

This search for prayer therefore is the defining challenge of our lives, the only reliable hope for meaning. The moment we are granted access to this authentic prayer we finally know that God is for us and that nothing ever will separate us from the love of God:

What then are we to say? If God is for us, who can be against us? . . . Who will separate us from the love of

[8] cf. Jn 16.13.
[9] Jn 14.16, 26; 15.26; 16.7; 1 Jn 2.1.

Christ? . . . I am convinced that neither death, nor life, nor angels, nor rulers, nor things present, nor things to come, nor powers, nor height, nor depth, nor anything else in all creation, will be able to separate us from the love of God in Christ Jesus our Lord.[10]

These confident words of Paul are the natural conclusion to this book. If we seem to have talked a lot about prayer, and yet to have given few practical indications on how to do it, the reasons should be clear by now: the way we pray is entirely free, exquisitely personal – each individual's way of praying is unique, as unique as one's DNA. All personal relationships are unrepeatable. Keeping this in mind, a few brief directions might prove useful. The best we have to offer are these: keep it simple, keep it short, keep it frequent, keep it real.

Keep it simple. A sentence, a cry, a word are enough. This is what the Psalms teach us – and they are the prayers that the people of Israel cherished most, believing them to have been inspired by God. Open the book of Psalms at random and you will find a treasure of short sentences to give voice to any possible existential situation, to convert any possible feeling into prayer.

[10] Cf. Rom. 8.31–39.

Trust: 'O Lord my God I take refuge in you.'[11] Joy: 'I will praise you O God with all my heart.'[12] Gratitude: 'You anoint my head with oil, my cup overflows.'[13] Distress: 'Answer me when I call to you O God, give me relief in my distress.'[14] Anger: 'You are God my stronghold, why have you rejected me?'[15] Despair: 'My God, my God, why have you forsaken me?'[16] Love: 'I love you O Lord, my strength, my rock, my fortress.'[17]

This list could go on for ever . . . Once you find the sentence that best expresses what you are going through in your life, what you are feeling, then just repeat it, gently, for as long as it sustains your prayer, whether for just five minutes or for longer. You will find that the more you repeat this sentence with your heart, the more it becomes meaningful, it expands, it is mysteriously filled from within. You know that the Father is listening to you and that through that word he is comforting you, reassuring you, healing you.

Keep it short. Prayer should last only as long as your inner urge for it does – your need, your feeling, your

[11] Ps. 7.1.
[12] Ps. 86.12.
[13] Ps. 23.5.
[14] Ps. 4.1.
[15] Ps. 43.2.
[16] Ps. 22.1.
[17] Ps. 18.1–2.

desire. It is not its length that matters but its intensity. This intensity will, of itself, slowly, progressively, make you want to carry on longer and longer, and persevere in prayer. And even when you have to go back to your activities, this prayer somehow remains with you in the background in the form of a peace, a joy, a calm, that nothing can take away from you.

Keep it frequent. No need to set your alarm to remind you when to pray. Your heart will prompt you. You will think: 'I can't right now, I am working.' And yet try to stop just a second and say it, *say it to God*: 'I don't have time, but I love you' – a smile will immediately lighten your face, joy and peace will fill your heart. It will have taken ten seconds of your precious time. This smile and this joy are addictive; you will do it more and more often, it will become a habit.

Keep it real. If you have had the patience to read this far you will know what I mean. Nothing of what you do, think, love, hate, suffer, enjoy, hope, fear, dread, desire – nothing is unworthy of God – there is nothing that you cannot convert into prayer. There is one rule, one method, one secret, one simple and infallible way to achieve this: just *say it to God*.

AFTERWORD
Michael Casey OCSO

In one of his precious statements about prayer, Jesus makes the surprising recommendation that we should pray without discernment, not making a judgement (Mk 11.23). So surprising is this statement that, even though we find the same admonition in the Epistle of James (Jas. 1.6), it is usually not adequately translated. The text of Mark reads: 'Amen I say to you that if anyone says to this mountain, "Be lifted up and cast into the sea," and does not judge in his heart but believes that what he says will happen, so it will be for him.'[1] Usually the verb *diakrinein* is translated in these texts as 'hesitate' or 'doubt'. There could be several causes of hesitation or doubt, but in this case the reluctance to believe comes from spending too much time weighing up the possibilities before committing oneself to make a request. Instead of saying it to God we attempt to filter our prayer before sending it, making sure the content is respectable and the manner of expression appropriate.

[1] All translations are the author's own.

Many people seem to confuse God with Queen Victoria of England. Of Queen Victoria it is known that not only was she queen of an empire on which the sun never set, but she was also the mother of a large family. Her maternal role was held up to the mothers of the British Empire for their admiration and imitation. Each day she would spend an hour with her children, holding the babies, playing with the children and asking the older ones what they had learned in school. What she didn't know, but we do, is that for the children the whole day revolved around this hour spent with their mother. They all arrived rested and washed and fed. The older ones were rehearsed in the answers they had to give. No doubt Her Majesty was gratified to see how content and polite and dutiful her children were, and it was a pleasant time for all. But this is scarcely what motherhood is about. Real mothers have to deal with children who are tired and cranky, sick or anxious, disobedient and sulky. The nature of maternal love is shown in how a mother responds to these negativities without rejecting her children or withholding her love. A real mother's love is exceedingly robust; it can cope with anything. This is an infinitely better picture of God than Queen Victoria.

Jesus was at pains to remind us often of the Father's universal and unconditional love. 'God causes the sun to rise on the evil and the good, and sends rain on the righteous and the unrighteous' (Mt. 5.45). 'God is kind to the ungrateful and wicked' (Lk. 6.35). We do not have to disguise our reality so as to appear before God as somehow better than we are. We do not have to turn our prayer into a well-rehearsed theatrical performance. It was for this playacting (the base meaning of the word translated as 'hypocrisy') that Jesus criticized the Pharisees. We are to come before God just as we are – not so much because that is something wonderful, but because God's acceptance is all-embracing. No matter what we do we cannot relocate ourselves to a zone outside God's love. All too often our difficulties in prayer come simply from a notion of God that does not do justice to the robust vigour of divine mercy. As Julian of Norwich wrote, '[God's] love is hard and marvellous, for it cannot and will not be broken for trespasses.' Our personal history can never become an obstacle to our access to God. On the contrary, it is the springboard from which the desire of our hearts leaps beyond self to the infinity of the spiritual world.

Luigi Gioia writes with great eloquence and from the standpoint of experience. Because it derives from reflection on the New Testament and has such a strong but subtle theological base, *Say it to God* will be a welcome source of instruction and consolation to many who feel the need to freshen their approach to God and their practice of prayer.

A NOTE ON THE AUTHOR

Luigi Gioia is Professor of Systematic Theology at the Pontifical University of Sant'Anselmo in Rome and Research Associate of the Von Hügel Institute (Cambridge). In the past four years he has preached spiritual retreats in the UK, France, USA, Canada, Australia, Korea, China, Philippines and he has published widely in scholarly reviews. He is currently Visiting Scholar of the Divinity Faculty at Cambridge University.

A NOTE ON THE TYPE

The text of this book is set in Perpetua. This typeface is an adaptation of a style of letter that had been popularised for monumental work in stone by Eric Gill. Large scale drawings by Gill were given to Charles Malin, a Parisian punch-cutter, and his hand-cut punches were the basis for the font issued by Monotype. First used in a private translation called 'The Passion of Perpetua and Felicity', the italic was originally called Felicity.